TOM JONES'
HOOD'S
TEXAS BRIGADE
sketch book

**INTRODUCTION BY
COLONEL HAROLD B. SIMPSON**

COPYRIGHT 1988
BY
TOM JONES

LIBRARY OF CONGRESS CATALOG CARD NUMBER
88-80596

ISBN 0-912172-34-7

FIRST PRINTING MARCH 1988
750 COPIES

PUBLISHED BY
HILL COLLEGE PRESS
HILLSBORO, TEXAS

TO MY OWN LITTLE GROUP OF
DIEHARD REBELS
(EACH IN THEIR OWN WAY)

♡ *Marie* ♡

Nonnie   Bill   Charles   Lavinia

Leisha   LynnLee   James   Marie   Katy

Preface

Hood's Texas Brigade consisted of the following Texas regiments and at different times other units, they were —

1st. Texas Infantry Regiment
4th. Texas Infantry Regiment
5th. Texas Infantry Regiment
3rd. Arkansas Infantry Regiment
18th. Georgia Infantry Regiment
Hampton's So. Carolina Legion
(Infantry Battalion)
1st. No. Carolina Artillery Regiment
(Rowan Artillery, Co. D)

In this sketch book those units that are not from Texas are not included. This is not an omission that is desirable. All of them served with great distinction and they are part and parcel of the brigade's proud fighting record. All of their descendents, both lineal and lateral, are most welcome to become members in the reactivated Hood's Texas Brigade Association.

The only reasons that they are not shown in this sketch book are the lack of contemporary pictorial material available to the artist and the time element required to collect same.

Acknowledgments

Over the past several years various people involved in civil war portrayals whether in print, paint, sculpture, drama or reenactments have made inquiries into my files as to the "look" of Hood's Texas Brigade. Of course, other than my children, I am not the source of anything. The material that I have collected has been invariably sought out from the best sources available to me. Institutions and individuals have been most helpful and I am grateful to them.

First and foremost would be Colonel Harold B. Simpson founder of the Confederate Research Center at Hill Junior College and the driving genius behind the reactivation of Hood's Texas Brigade Association. Colonel Simpson has authored four magnificent volumes on this great fighting unit. Michael Robert Green of the Texas State Archives supplied invaluable data on the battle flags used by the brigade. I would like to thank Casey Edward Greene, Rosenberg Library, Galveston; Ms Rebecca Ansell, The Museum of the Confederacy, Richmond; and Mrs Sam G. Cook, The Texas Confederate Museum, Austin.

Published books, diaries, letters and individuals have been consulted, not the least of which were actual Confederate veterans who graciously answered the many questions of an admiring boy.

Tom

INTRODUCTION

If anyone is qualified to compile a sketchbook on Hood's Texas Brigade, it is Tom Jones. Tom is not only a nationally known artist and sculptor of great reputation, but he has a close connection with the famous fighting unit that served under Robert E. Lee. His great grandfather, Walter Scott Jones, served in Company G, Fourth Texas Infantry Regiment, which was recruited in Grimes County, Texas, and was known as "The Grimes County Greys." Private Walter Scott Jones would be killed at Gaines' Mill on June 27, 1862. Too, Tom Jones has served as the president of Hood's Texas Brigade Association (1972-1976) that was reactivated in 1967 by the Confederate Research Center of Hill College. To become a member of this association, one must be a direct or collateral descendant of a member of the Brigade. Following the war there were hundreds such veterans groups organized, however, Hood's Texas Brigade Association is the **only** Civil War veterans association, North or South, to be reactivated to date.

In his **Sketchbook**, Jones catches the drama of the Old Brigade; the dedicated enlisted and officer personnel who served in it; the irregular, sometimes scruffy uniforms; and the crude accouterments and equipment worn and carried by its young, hard-fighting men. A section of his book is reserved for drawings of the Brigade's battle standards, torn and bullet-riddled; all are faithfully portrayed. Thus, the Brigade is brought to life through the eyes and keen hands of a master artist. To create the personnel sketches, Jones used, from the archives of the Confederate Research Center, actual photographs of Hood's Texans. Noted in these pictures are a certain cockiness, an air of self-assurance and even defiance, particularly in the visage of the officers. All of these expressions are faultlessly captured by the artist's pencil. Sketches of all ranks of Texans have been faithfully reproduced — privates, non-commissioned officers, and officers, their uniforms and their flags, as they were at war 125 years ago. Jones, a master wood-carver, devotes the fourth section of his sketchbook to the carving of military statuettes and illustrates this section with several of his best known works.

Hood's Texas Brigade Sketchbook will be of particular interest and value to the growing number of re-enactors, those present-day Billy Yanks and Johnny Rebs who weekly relive and refight the War Between the States. Not only is this fast developing hobby intriguing Americans, but young men of Great Britain, Australia, Belgium and Germany, in particular, have become interested in re-fighting the American Civil War. While the re-enacting groups in the United States are sympathetically split between the North and the South, almost without exception foreign re-enactors have embraced the Confederate cause. The companies and regiments of Hood's Texas Brigade appear to be among those favored by the current Confederate hobbyists. As the director of the Confederate Research Center and Museum at Hill College, I receive numerous inquiries from within the states and from abroad asking about the uniforms, equipment, and flags that certain companies of Hood's Texas Brigade wore or carried. My replies to many of these questions, I am sure, did not answer these inquiries satisfactorily. As an old Chinese philosopher once said, "One picture is worth 10,000 words." Now we have a "picture book" to provide accurate answers.

James Thomas "Tom" Jones has worked in many fields of art: design, painting, sculptor, wood carving, illustrating, and cartooning. In all of these fields he has carved out a national reputation for himself and his work. Among other things, he has been a cowboy, a soldier, and a teacher. Tom has combined his many talents over the years to produce some five hundred pieces of art work housed in various private and public collections across the United States. The largest permanent collection of his water colors and wood sculptures is located in the "Sam Houston Room" of the Victoria Bank and Trust Company of Victoria, Texas. Jones has contributed art work for several books published by the Hill College Press, in particular the best seller, **Audie Murphy, American**

Soldier. In this new book, **Hood's Texas Brigade Sketchbook**, military art is presented at its very best.

In selecting Hood's Texas Brigade to sketch, Jones chose one of the best known fighting units in the Confederate Army. No other brigade, North or South, was involved in such sustained fighting and suffered as many casualties as did Hood's Texans. The war record of this famed Brigade was a gallant and a glorious one. It was a record written in blood, battlesmoke, and bandages from the swamps of Chickahominy to the rocks of Devil's Den and to the scrub oaks of the Wilderness. Hood's Texas Brigade fought in all of the major battles engaged in by the Army of Northern Virginia except Chancellorsville, and it more than made up for missing this battle by fighting at Chickamauga with the Army of Tennessee. Hood's Texans helped Lee win his first battle of the war at Gaines' Mill and they remained steadfast and defiant to the end at Appomattox.

The Brigade fought in thirty-eight (38) engagements from Eltham's Landing, May 7, 1862, to Appomattox Courthouse, April 9, 1865. The Texans participated in six of the greatest battles fought in the war and suffered some 3,500 casualties. At the battle of Antietam (September 17, 1862), the deadliest single day of battle in modern warfare, the First Texas Infantry Regiment of the Brigade suffered the greatest casualty rate of any regiment, Confederate or Federal, for a single days fighting during the war. The regiment had 82.3% of its men killed, wounded, or missing during the battle. It fought until it was literally decimated.

It is estimated that some 5,300 men served in the three Texas regiments and the one Arkansas regiment (the Third Arkansas) that composed the Brigade for most of the war. At Appomattox Courthouse on April 12, 1865, only 617 of this number, less than 12% of those who had enlisted in the Brigade, were left to be paroled. Thus, some 4,700 members of the Brigade had been killed in battle, had died of disease, had been invalided home due to prolonged sieges of sickness and crippling wounds, or had been discharged for being either too old or too young, but few had deserted.

    Certainly the soldiers of Hood's Texas Brigade exemplified the inscription chisled on the side of the Confederate Memorial in the Arlington National Cemetery—

> Not for fame or record, nor for place or rank,
> Nor lured by ambition or goaded by necessity,
> But in simple obedience to duty as they understood it;
> These men suffered all, sacrificed all, endured all; and died.

These are the men and the times that Tom Jones has brought to life with his pencils and his chisels.

                                            Harold B. Simpson
                                            Hill College
                                            March, 1988

Contents

Section A
PHOTOGRAPHIC INTERPRETATIONS

Section B
UNIFORMS & ACCOUTERMENTS

Section C
BATTLE STANDARDS

Section D
MILITARY STATUETTES

SECTION A

PHOTOGRAPHIC INTERPRETATIONS

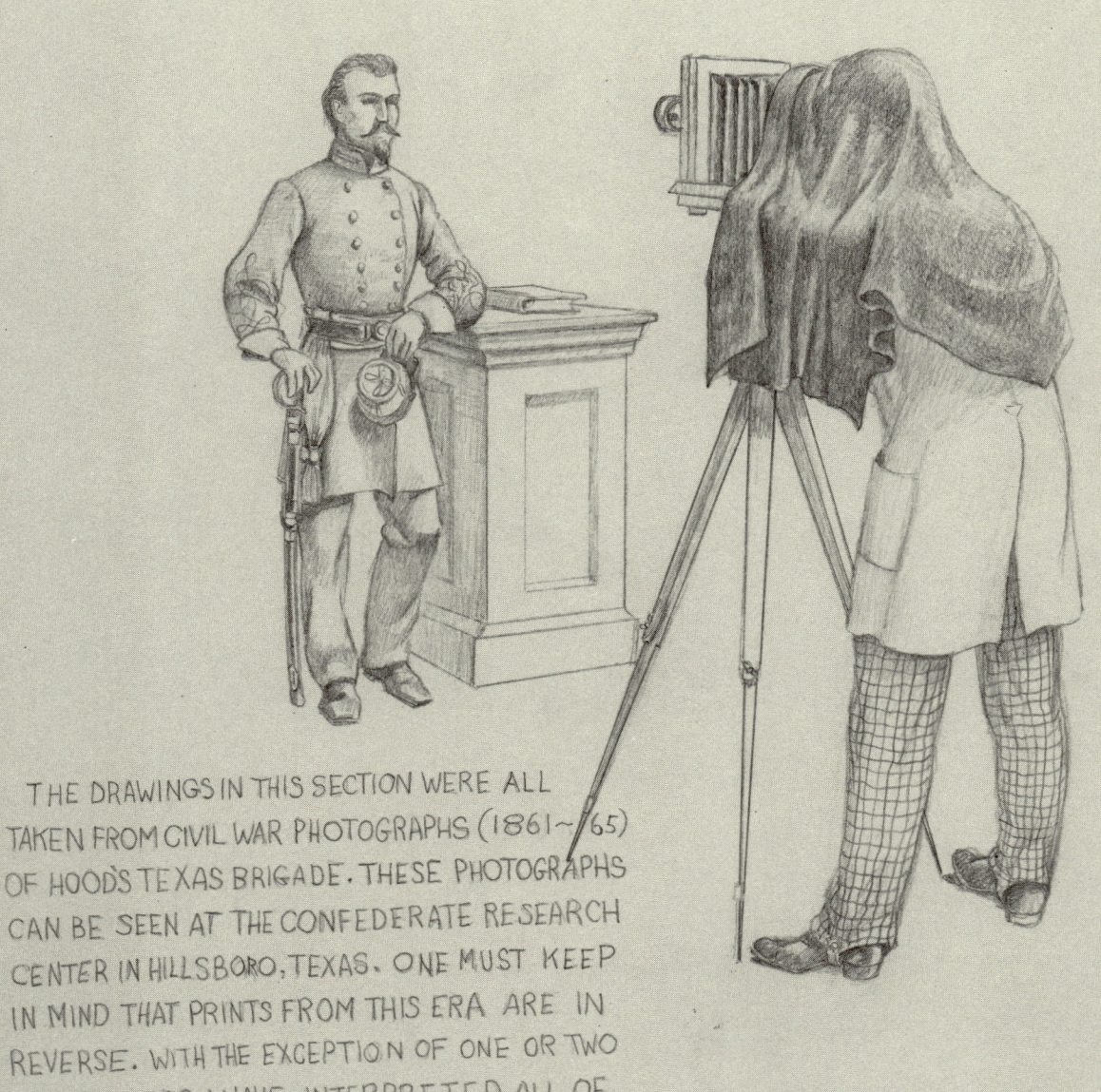

THE DRAWINGS IN THIS SECTION WERE ALL TAKEN FROM CIVIL WAR PHOTOGRAPHS (1861~'65) OF HOOD'S TEXAS BRIGADE. THESE PHOTOGRAPHS CAN BE SEEN AT THE CONFEDERATE RESEARCH CENTER IN HILLSBORO, TEXAS. ONE MUST KEEP IN MIND THAT PRINTS FROM THIS ERA ARE IN REVERSE. WITH THE EXCEPTION OF ONE OR TWO NOTED CASES, I HAVE INTERPRETED ALL OF THE PRINTS EXACTLY AS SHOWN.

1ST. TEX. VOL. INF. REGT.

CO. A
MARION RIFLES
MARION COUNTY, TEXAS

CO. B
LIVINGSTON GUARDS
LIVINGSTON, POLK COUNTIES, TEXAS

CO. C
PALMER GUARDS
HARRIS COUNTY, TEXAS

CO. D
STAR RIFLES
MARION COUNTY, TEXAS

CO. E
MARSHALL GUARDS
HARRISON COUNTY, TEXAS

CO. F
WOODVILLE RIFLES
TYLER COUNTY, TEXAS

CO. G
REAGAN GUARDS
ANDERSON COUNTY, TEXAS

CO. H
TEXAS GUARDS
ANDERSON COUNTY, TEXAS

CO. I
CROCKETT SOUTHRONS
HOUSTON COUNTY, TEXAS

CO. K
TEXAS INVINCIBLES
SAN AUGUSTINE COUNTY, TEXAS

CO. L
LONE STAR RIFLES
GALVESTON COUNTY, TEXAS

CO. M
SUMTER LIGHT INFANTRY
TRINITY COUNTY, TEXAS

CO. D 1ST. TEX.
STAR RIFLES
MARION COUNTY, TEXAS

3 Lt. C.R. CARTRIGHT AND FIVE OF THE SEVEN OLIVER BROTHERS, ALL OF WHOM WERE MEMBERS OF CO. D 1ST. TEX. THEY WERE A.C. OLIVER, F.T. OLIVER, H.B. OLIVER, JOHN. A. OLIVER, S.W. OLIVER, W.A.T. OLIVER AND WM. H. OLIVER. FOUR SURVIVED THE WAR.

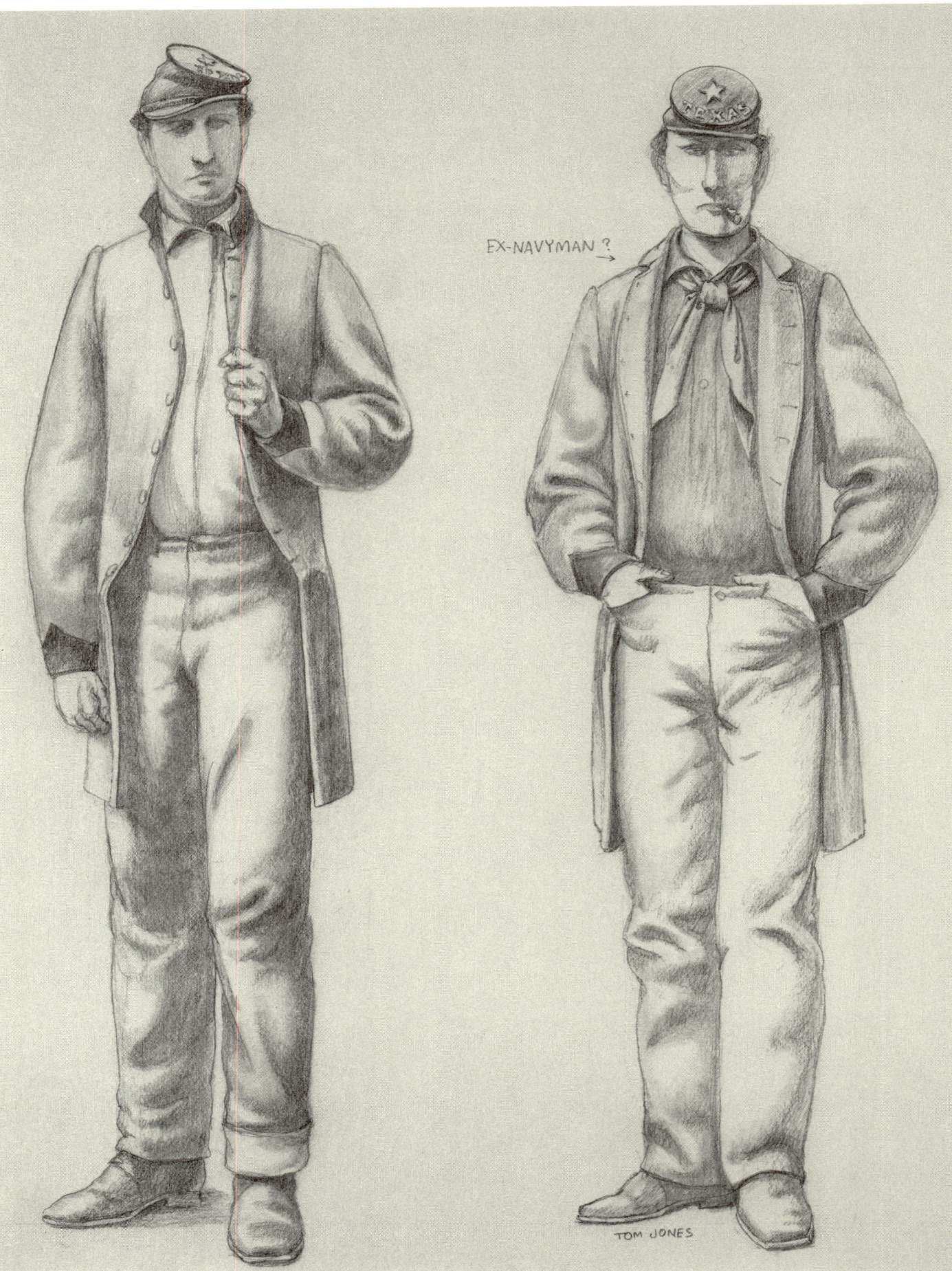

4TH. TEX. VOL. INF. REGT.

CO. A
HARDIMAN RIFLES
GOLIAD COUNTY, TEXAS

CO. B
TOM GREEN RIFLES
TRAVIS COUNTY, TEXAS

CO. C
ROBERTSON FIVE SHOOTERS
ROBERTSON COUNTY, TEXAS

CO. D
GUADALUPE RANGERS OR
KNIGHTS of GUADALUPE COUNTY
GUADALUPE COUNTY, TEXAS

CO. E
LONE STAR GUARDS
McLENNAN COUNTY, TEXAS

CO. F
MUSTANG GRAYS
BEXAR COUNTY, TEXAS

CO. G
GRIMES COUNTY GREYS
GRIMES COUNTY, TEXAS

CO. H
PORTER GUARDS
WALKER, GRIMES, MONTGOMERY,
& WASHINGTON COUNTIES, TEXAS

CO. I
NAVARRO RIFLES
NAVARRO, ELLIS, FREESTONE &
HILL COUNTIES, TEXAS

CO. K
SANDY POINT MOUNTED RIFLES
HENDERSON COUNTY, TEXAS

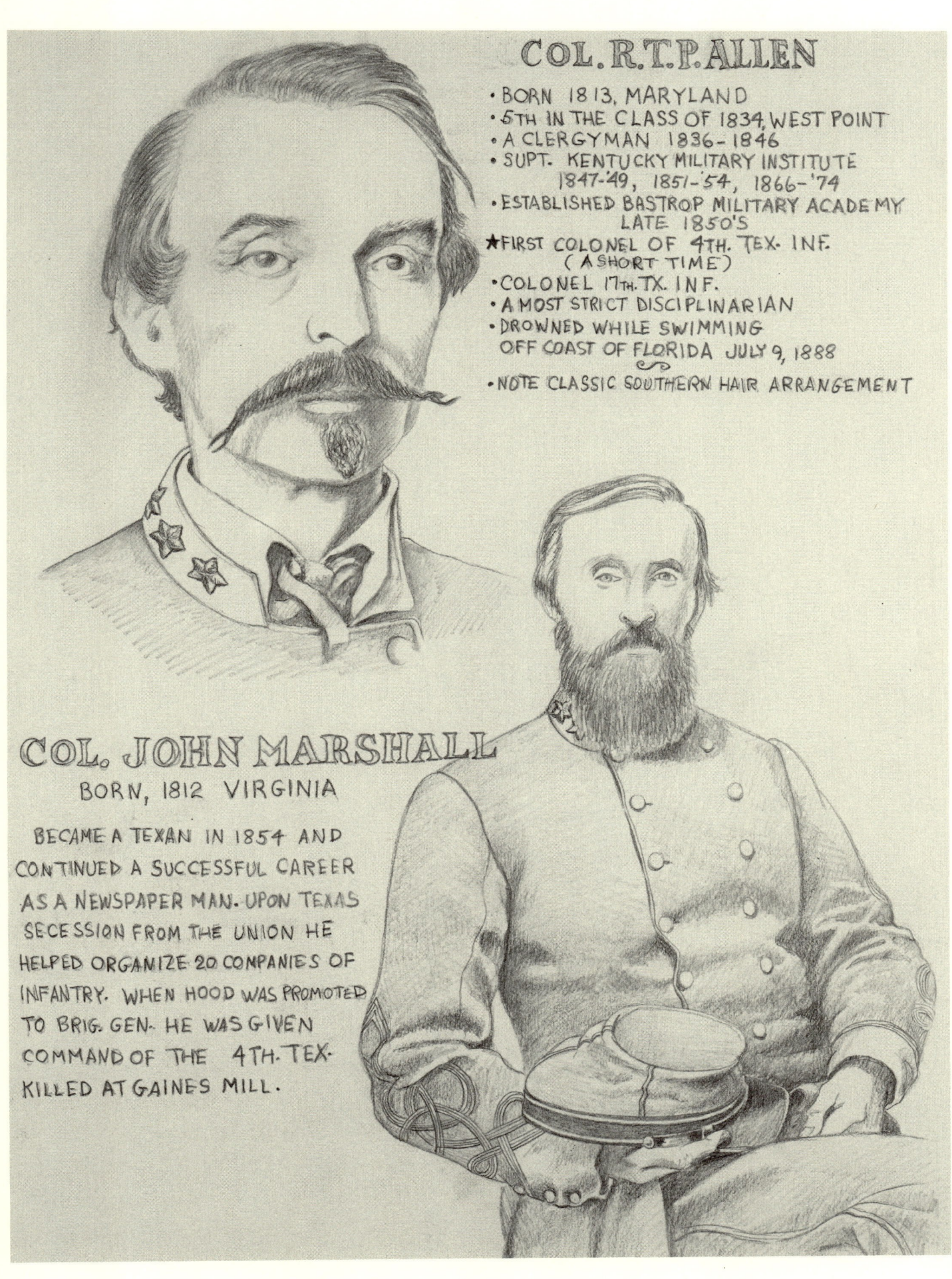

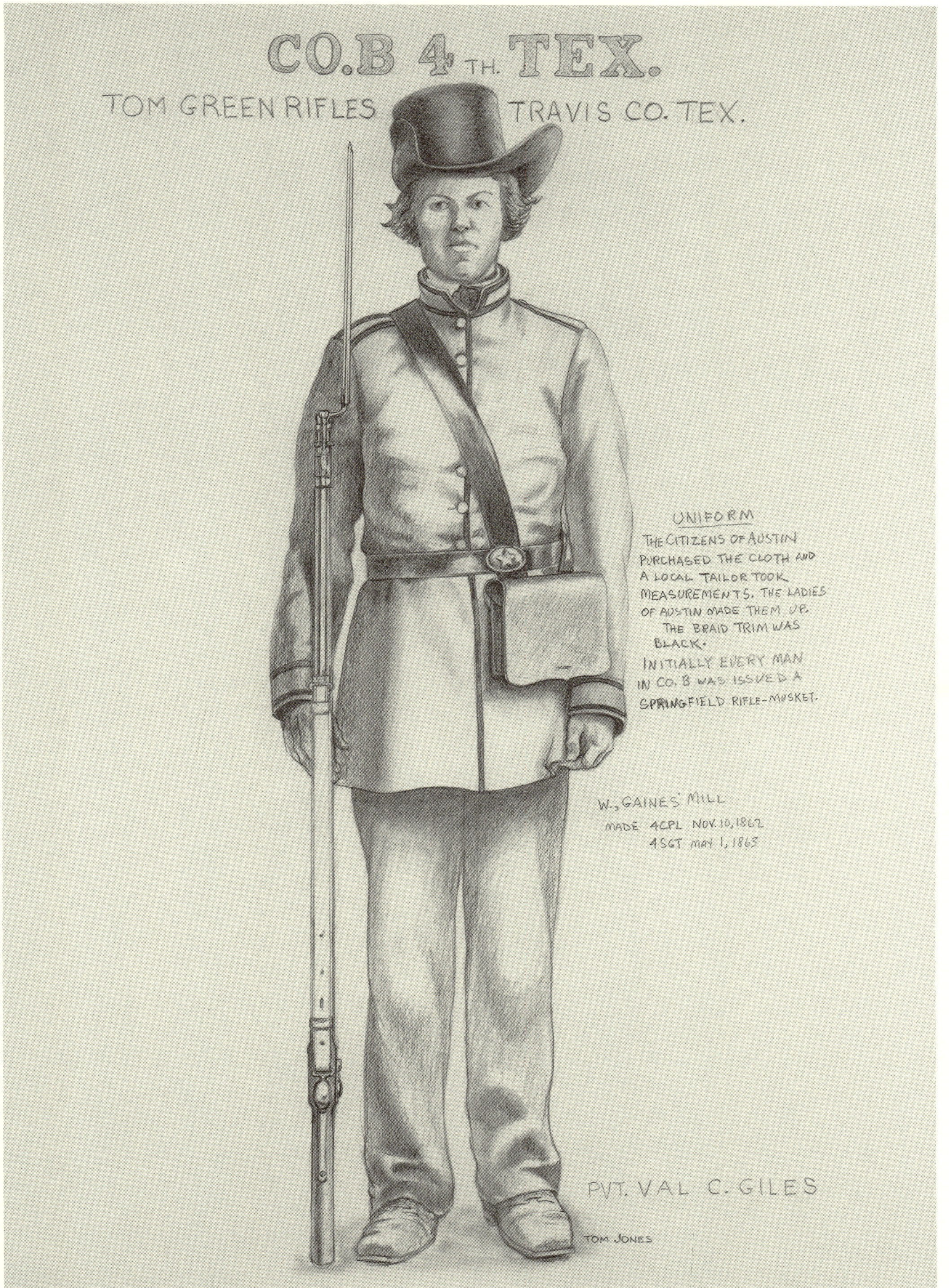
CO.B 4TH. TEX.
TOM GREEN RIFLES
TRAVIS CO. TEX.
UNIFORM
THE CITIZENS OF AUSTIN PURCHASED THE CLOTH AND A LOCAL TAILOR TOOK MEASUREMENTS. THE LADIES OF AUSTIN MADE THEM UP.
THE BRAID TRIM WAS BLACK.
INITIALLY EVERY MAN IN CO. B WAS ISSUED A SPRINGFIELD RIFLE-MUSKET.
W., GAINES' MILL
MADE 4CPL NOV. 10, 1862
4SGT MAY 1, 1863
PVT. VAL C. GILES
TOM JONES

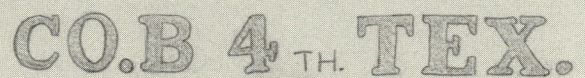

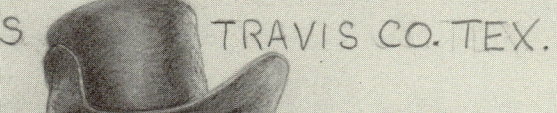

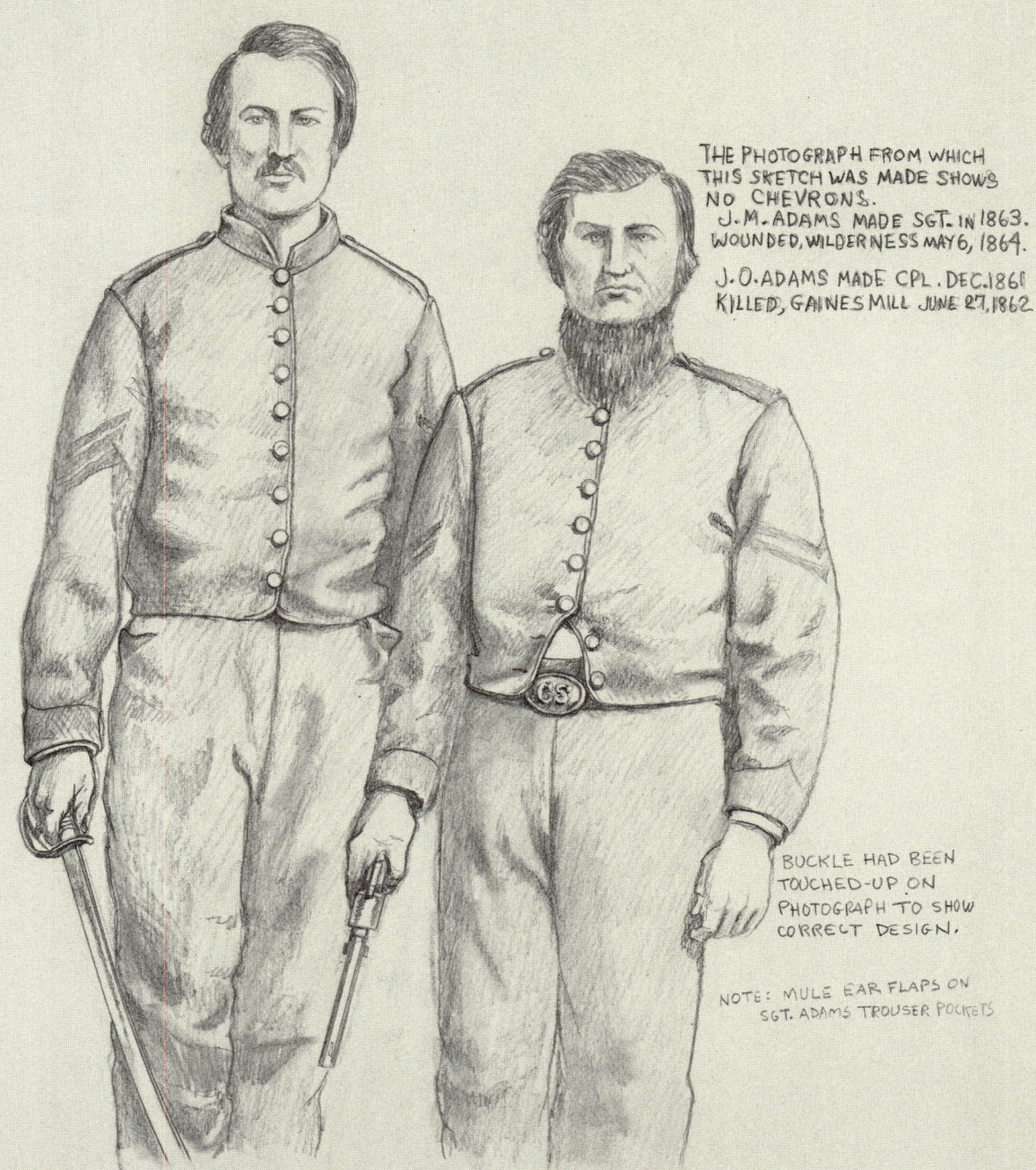

CO. E 4TH. TEX.
LONE STAR GUARDS
McLENNAN, CO., TEX.

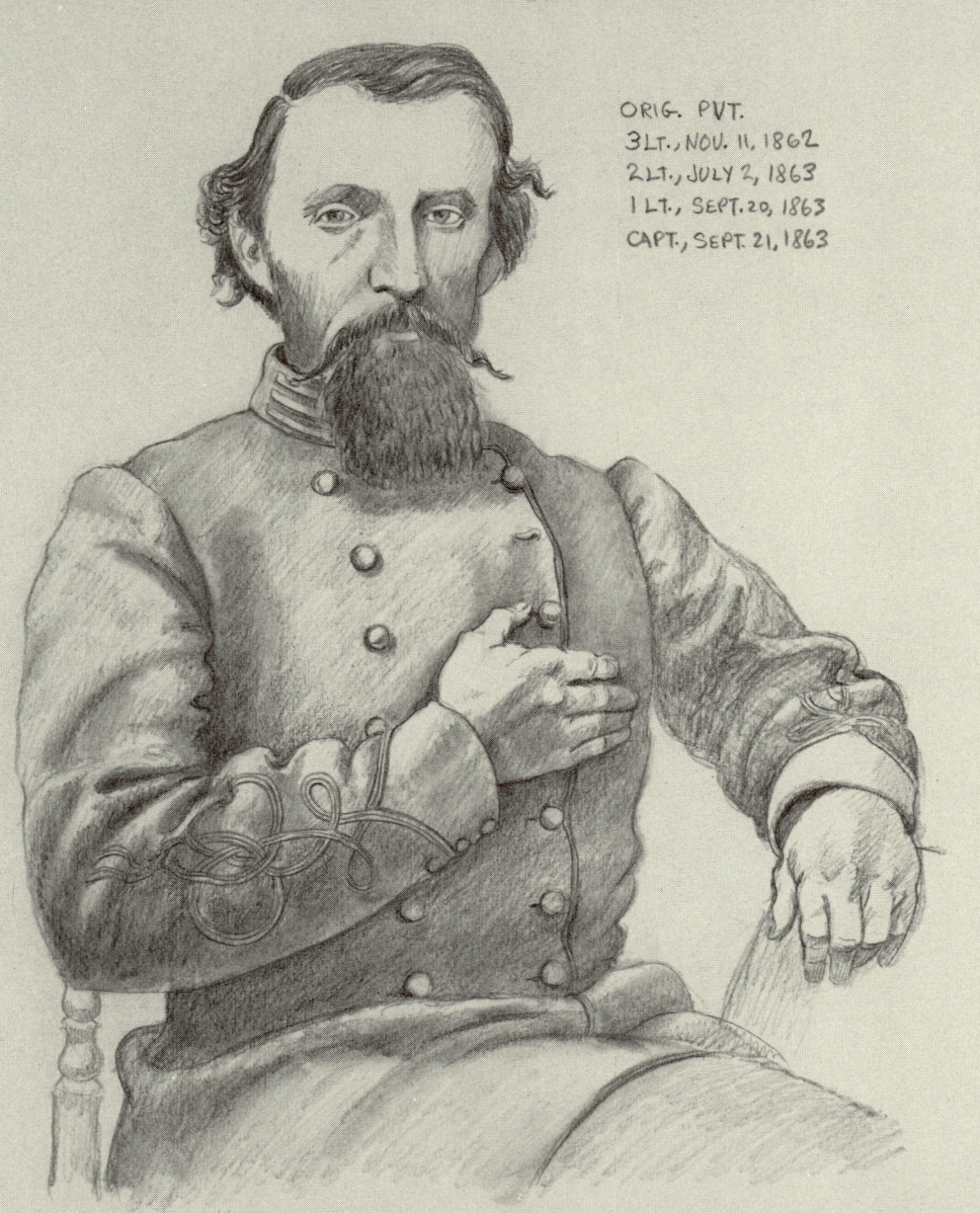

ORIG. PVT.
3 LT., NOV. 11, 1862
2 LT., JULY 2, 1863
1 LT., SEPT. 20, 1863
CAPT., SEPT. 21, 1863

CAPT. THOS. J. SELMAN

CO. G 4TH. TEX.
GRIMES CO. GREYS
GRIMES CO., TEX.

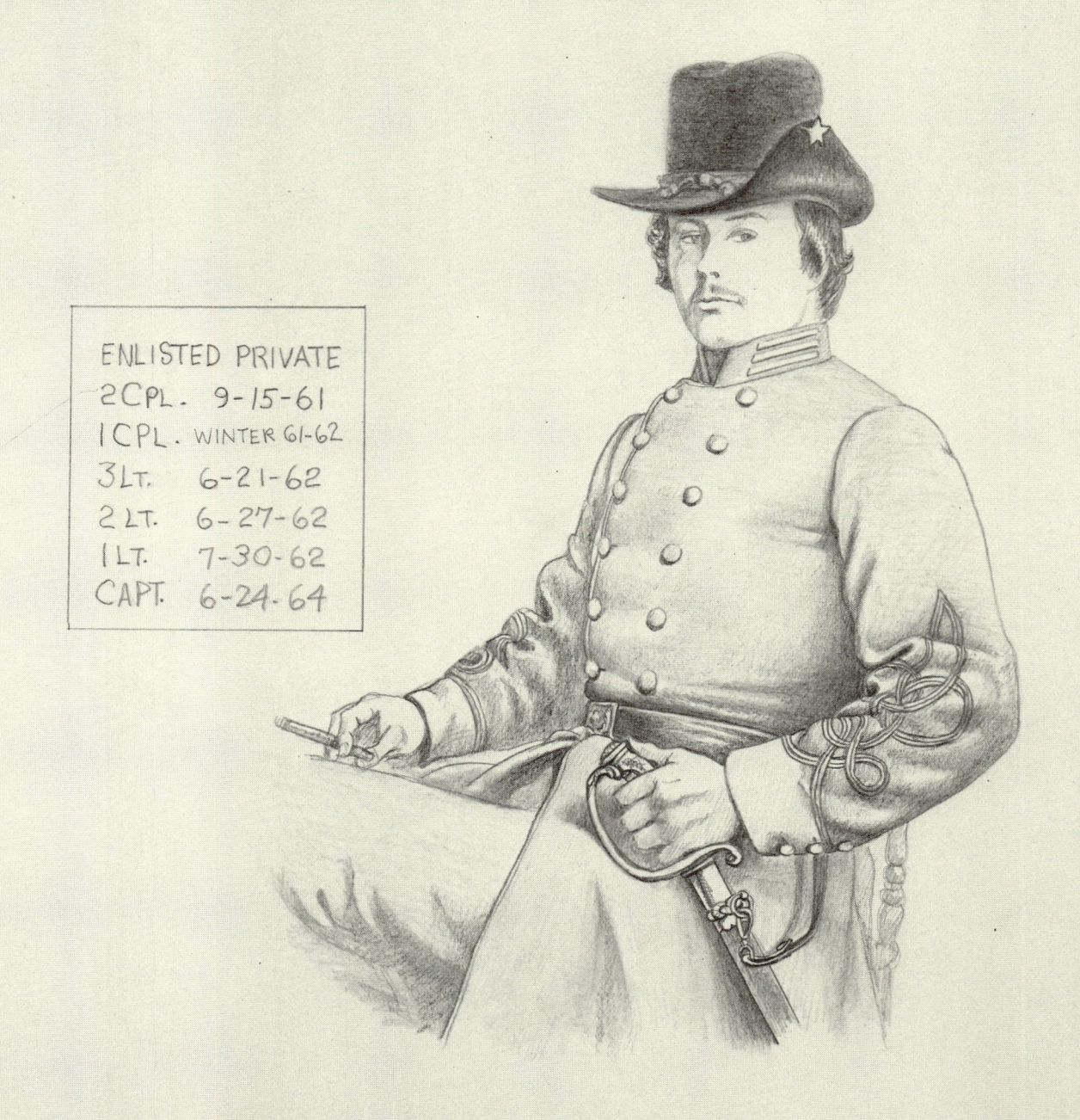

ENLISTED PRIVATE
2 CPL. 9-15-61
1 CPL. WINTER 61-62
3 LT. 6-21-62
2 LT. 6-27-62
1 LT. 7-30-62
CAPT. 6-24-64

CAPT. THOS. C. BUFFINGTON

CO. G 4TH TEX.
GRIMES COUNTY GREYS
GRIMES CO., TEX.

SINCE MANY OLD TIME TEXANS HAD A PREJUDICE AGAINST CARRYING CANTEENS, I WONDER WHAT SGT. BOOZER HAD IN HIS.
NOTE: BELT BUCKLE.

SGT. HUGH DICKSON BOOZER

CO. H 4TH. TEX.
PORTER GUARDS: WALKER CO., TEX.

EARLY SKETCH FROM A PHOTOGRAPH.

SINCE THE PHOTOGRAPHERS IN 1861 TRIED TO REARRANGE THE GEAR, I TRIED TO PUT IT BACK IN THIS SKETCH.

PVT. FRANK B. CHILTON

CO. I 4TH TEX.
NAVARRO RIFLES
NAVARRO COUNTY, TEX.

W. GAINE'S MILL

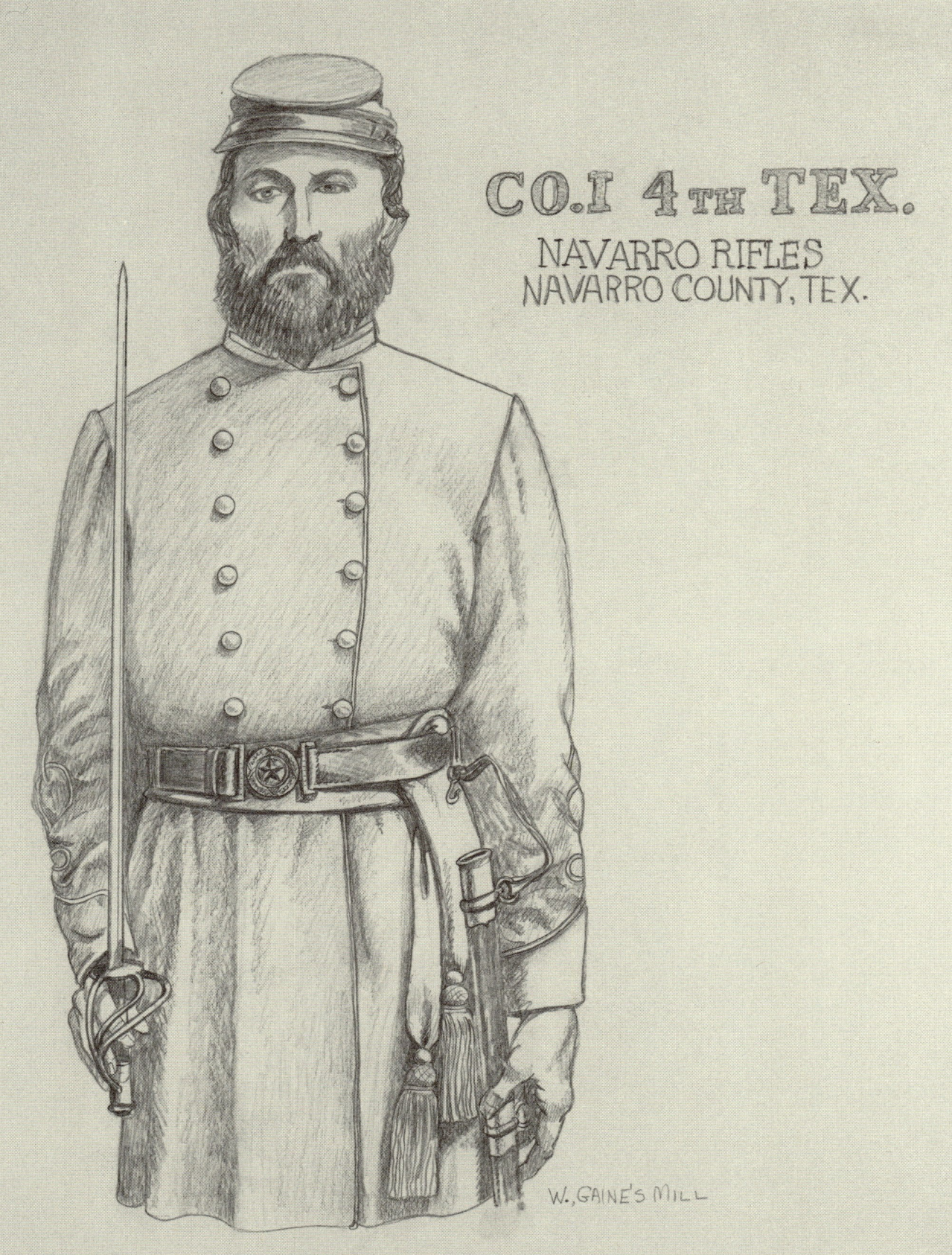

1LT. J. R. LOUGHRIDGE

CO. K 4TH TEX.
SANDY POINT MOUNTED RIFLES
HENDERSON CO., TEX.

AGAIN, THE ORIGINAL PHOTO WAS TAMPERED WITH. THE WORD "TEXAS" HAS BEEN PAINTED OVER AND RE LETTERED IN WHITE BECAUSE IN THE PHOTO IT READ, "SAXET"

THIS HANDSOME YOUNG CONFEDERATE LITERALLY GAVE HIS RIGHT ARM FOR THE — "NOBLE CAUSE."

3LT. WILLIAM D. RONNSAVALL

5TH. TEX. VOL. INF. REGT.

CO. A
BAYOU CITY GUARDS
HARRIS COUNTY, TEXAS

CO. B
NO LOCAL DESIGNATION
COLORADO COUNTY, TEXAS

CO. C
THE LEON HUNTERS
LEON COUNTY, TEXAS

CO. D
WAVERLY CONFEDERATES
WALKER COUNTY, TEXAS

CO. E
DIXIE BLUES
WASHINGTON COUNTY, TEXAS

CO. F
COMPANY INVINCIBLES
WASHINGTON COUNTY, TEXAS

CO. G
MILAM COUNTY GREYS
MILAM COUNTY, TEXAS

CO. H
TEXAS POLK RIFLES
POLK COUNTY, TEXAS

CO. I
TEXAS AIDES
WASHINGTON COUNTY, TEXAS

CO. K
POLK COUNTY FLYING ARTILLERY
POLK COUNTY, TEXAS

Brig. Gen. Jerome B. Robertson

ORIG. CAPT., CO. I 5TH. TEX.

PROM., LT-COL., OCT. 10, 1861

PROM., COL., JUNE 2, 1862
  TOOK CMD, 5TH. TEX. INF.
  W., GAINES' MILL
  W., 2ND MANASSAS

PROM., BRIG-GEN., NOV 1, 1862
  ASGND. CMD., HOOD'S TEX. BRIG.
  W., GETTYSBURG

COURT-MARTIALED, FEB. 25, 1864

ROBERTSON WAS COMMANDER OF HOOD'S TEX. BRIG. LONGER THAN ANY OTHER GENERAL.

TOM JONES

Col. James J. Archer

BVT. MAJ. FOR GALLANTRY, MEXICAN WAR: ORIG. CMDR. 5TH TEX. INF. REGT.
FEB. 20, 1862 - ASGND. CMD. TEX. BRIG.
MAR. 12, 1862 - RETURNED TO CMD. 5TH TEX. INF.
JUNE 3, 1862 - PROM. BRIG. GEN. &
　　　　　　　ASGND. CMD., HATTON'S TENN. BRIG.
JULY 1, 1863 - POW GETTYSBURG & CONFINED
　　　JOHNSON'S IS. PRISON CAMP - EXCHANGED SUMMER 1864
OCT. 24, 1864 - DIED RICHMOND

ARCHER WAS A CAPTAIN IN THE 9TH INF. U.S.A. BEFORE THE CIVIL WAR.

CO. A 5TH. TEX.
BAYOU CITY GUARDS
HARRIS CO. TEX.

CAPT. D.C. FARMER

CO. A 5TH TEX. INF.
BAYOU CITY GUARDS
HARRIS COUNTY, TEXAS

B. PUGH FULLER

ORIG. PVT. IN CO. A, 5 TEX.
NOV. 7, 1861 PROM. 3 LT. – JUNE 27, 1862 PROM. 2 LT.
SEPT. 1, 1863 PROM. 1 LT. – MAY 6, 1864 W. WILDERNESS.

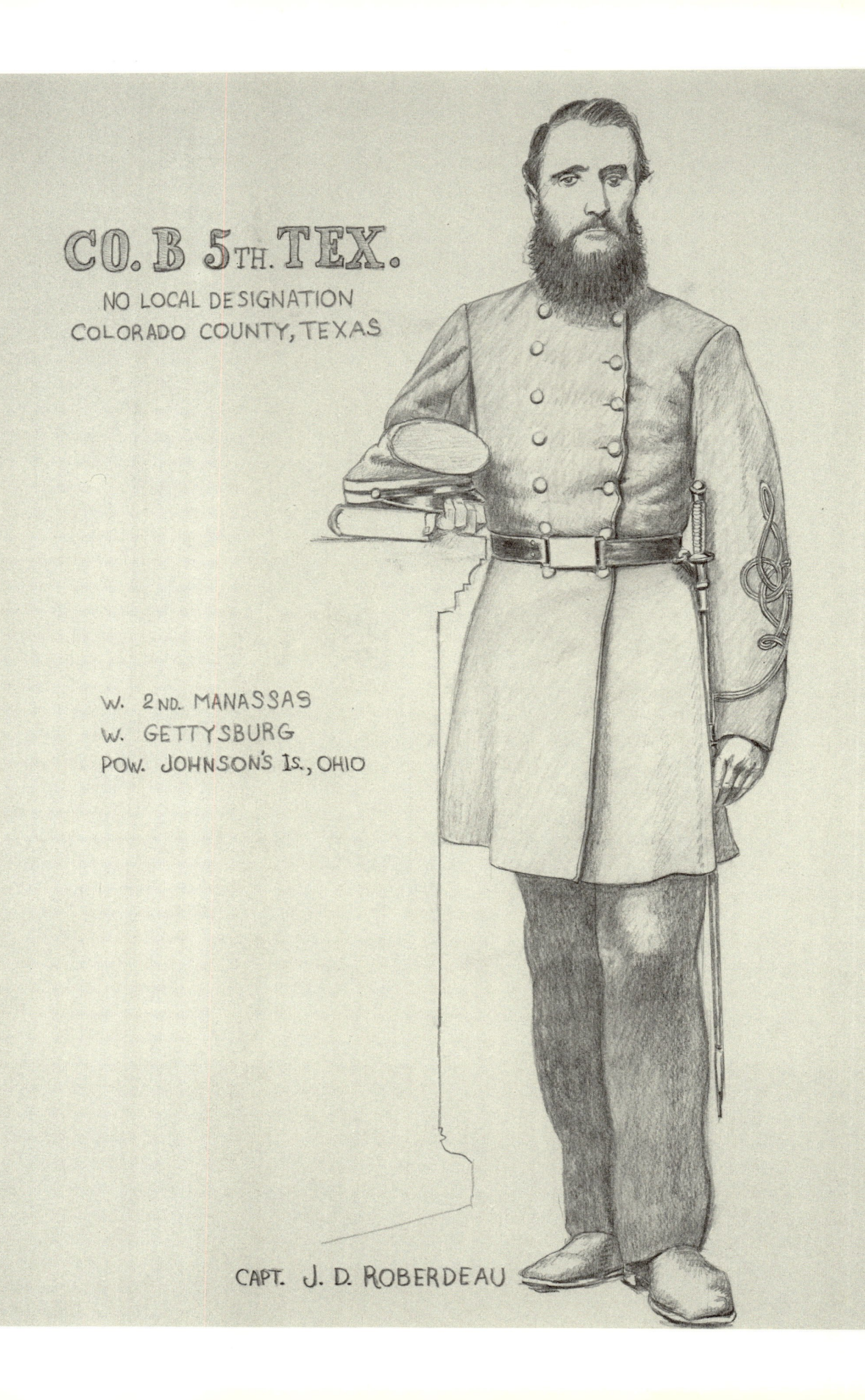

CO. B 5TH. TEX.
NO LOCAL DESIGNATION
COLORADO COUNTY, TEXAS

W. 2ND. MANASSAS
W. GETTYSBURG
POW. JOHNSON'S Is., OHIO

CAPT. J. D. ROBERDEAU

CO. E 5TH. TEX.
DIXIE BLUES
WASHINGTON CO., TEXAS

RUFUS K. FELDER, PVT.

MIERS M. FELDER, 2CPL.

CO. F 5TH. TEX.
COMPANY INVINCIBLES
WASHINGTON COUNTY, TEXAS

3 Lt. Bryan L. Pryor

CO. I 5TH. TEX.
TEXAS AIDES
WASHINGTON COUNTY, TEXAS

CAPT. TACITUS T. CLAY

SECTION B

UNIFORMS & ACCOUTERMENTS

U.S. ARMY FORAGE CAP M. 1858
SEVERAL PHOTOGRAPHS SHOW MEN OF THE 1ST. TEX. INF. WEARING THIS CAP WITH A SILVER STAR AND VARIOUS BRASS LETTERS ON TOP. THOSE WITH S.R.1. MUST BE FROM CO. D. 1ST. TEX., STAR RIFLES.

LT. BLUE W. GOLD BRAID

GRAY

LT. BLUE

D. BLUE

COLONEL'S KIPI

COMMON KIPI

REGULATION KIPI

VARIOUS CAMPAIGN HATS

OR SLOUCH HATS

BRASS BUTTONS →

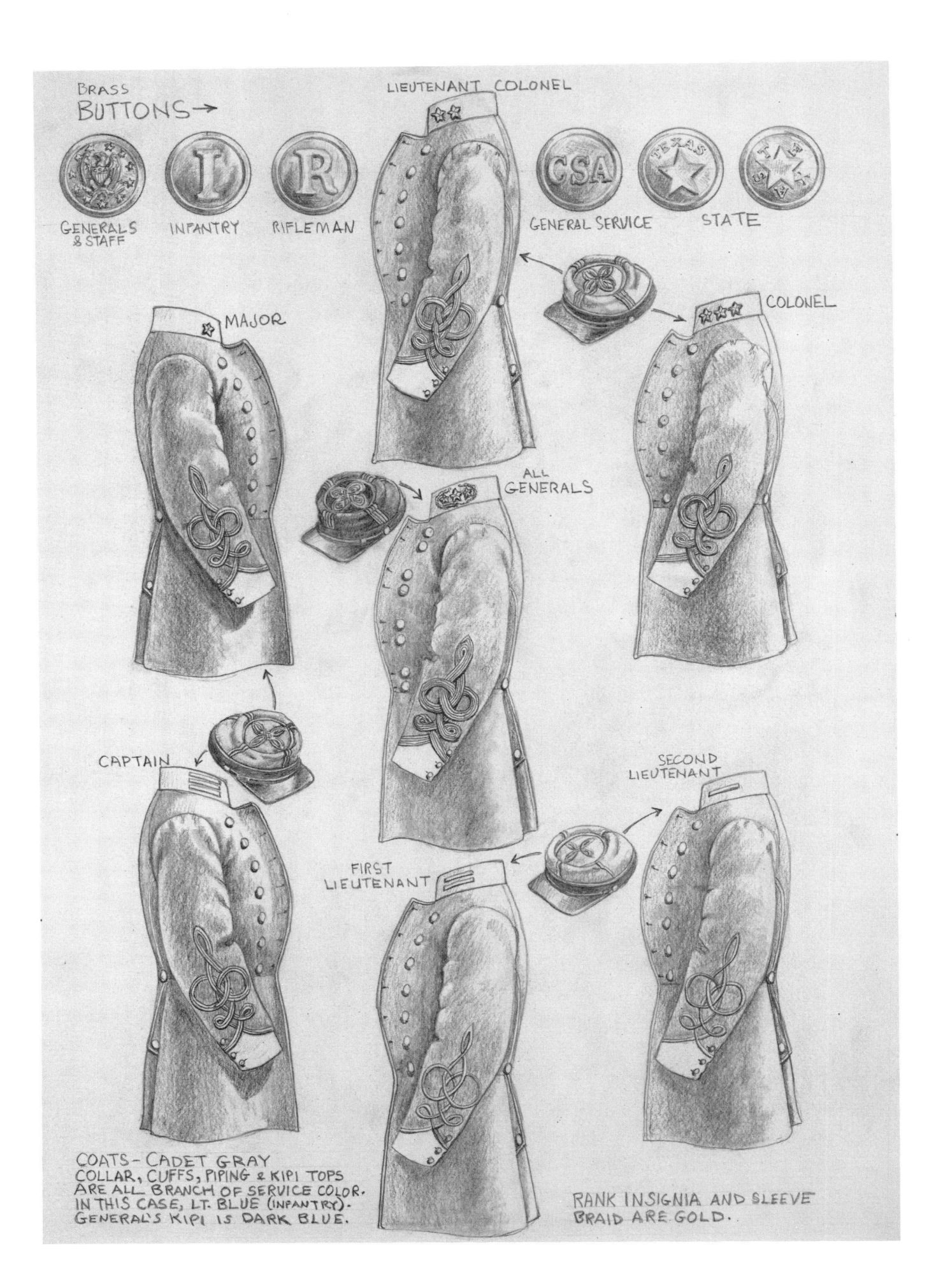

- GENERALS & STAFF
- INFANTRY
- RIFLEMAN
- GENERAL SERVICE
- STATE

LIEUTENANT COLONEL

MAJOR

COLONEL

ALL GENERALS

CAPTAIN

FIRST LIEUTENANT

SECOND LIEUTENANT

COATS - CADET GRAY
COLLAR, CUFFS, PIPING & KIPI TOPS ARE ALL BRANCH OF SERVICE COLOR. IN THIS CASE, LT. BLUE (INFANTRY). GENERAL'S KIPI IS DARK BLUE.

RANK INSIGNIA AND SLEEVE BRAID ARE GOLD.

Enlisted Men's Coats

1. Frock coat seen in many early (1861) photographs in various shades of gray.

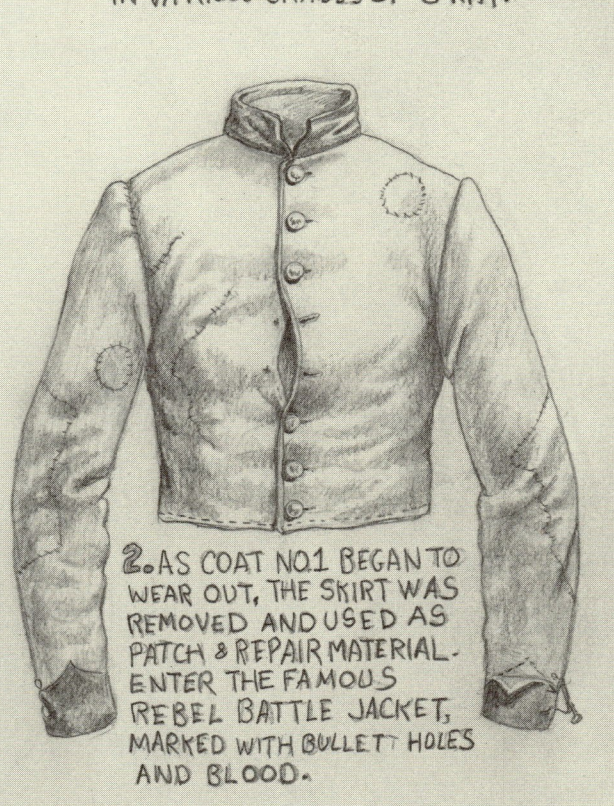

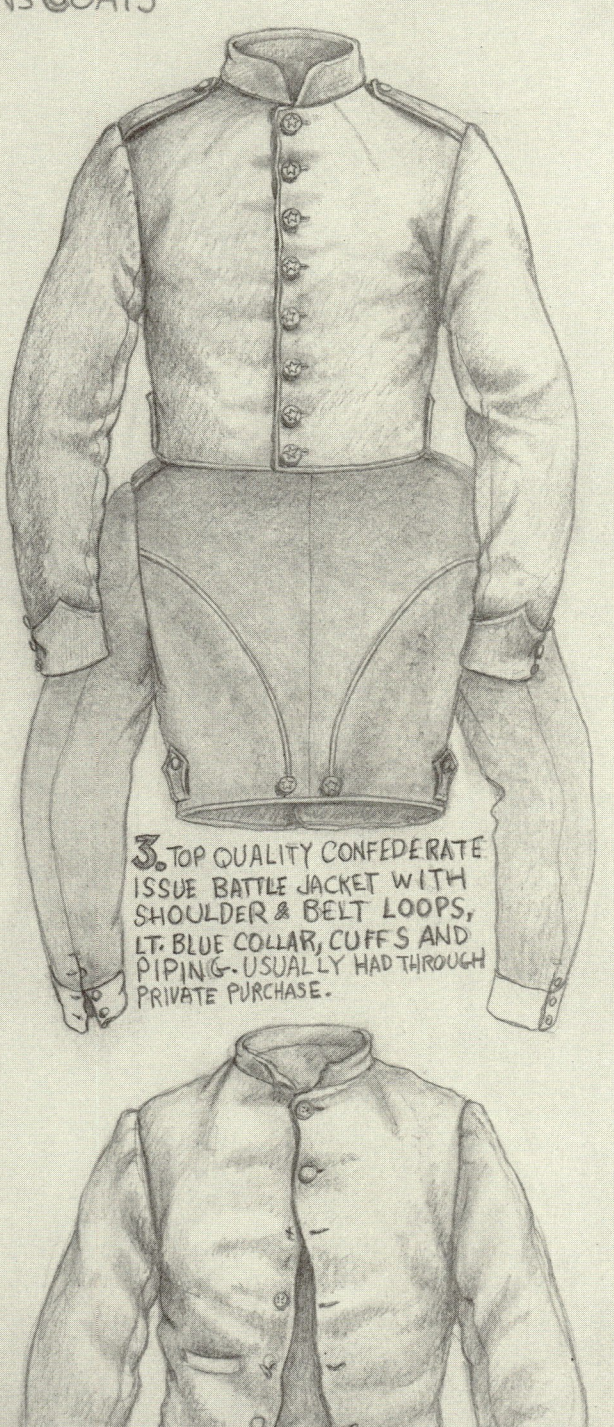

2. As coat No. 1 began to wear out, the skirt was removed and used as patch & repair material. Enter the famous rebel battle jacket, marked with bullet holes and blood.

3. Top quality Confederate issue battle jacket with shoulder & belt loops, lt. blue collar, cuffs and piping. Usually had through private purchase.

4. A cheaply made, no frills, plain, battle jacket. Common in the latter stages of the war, in various shades of brown, called butternut.

Chevrons

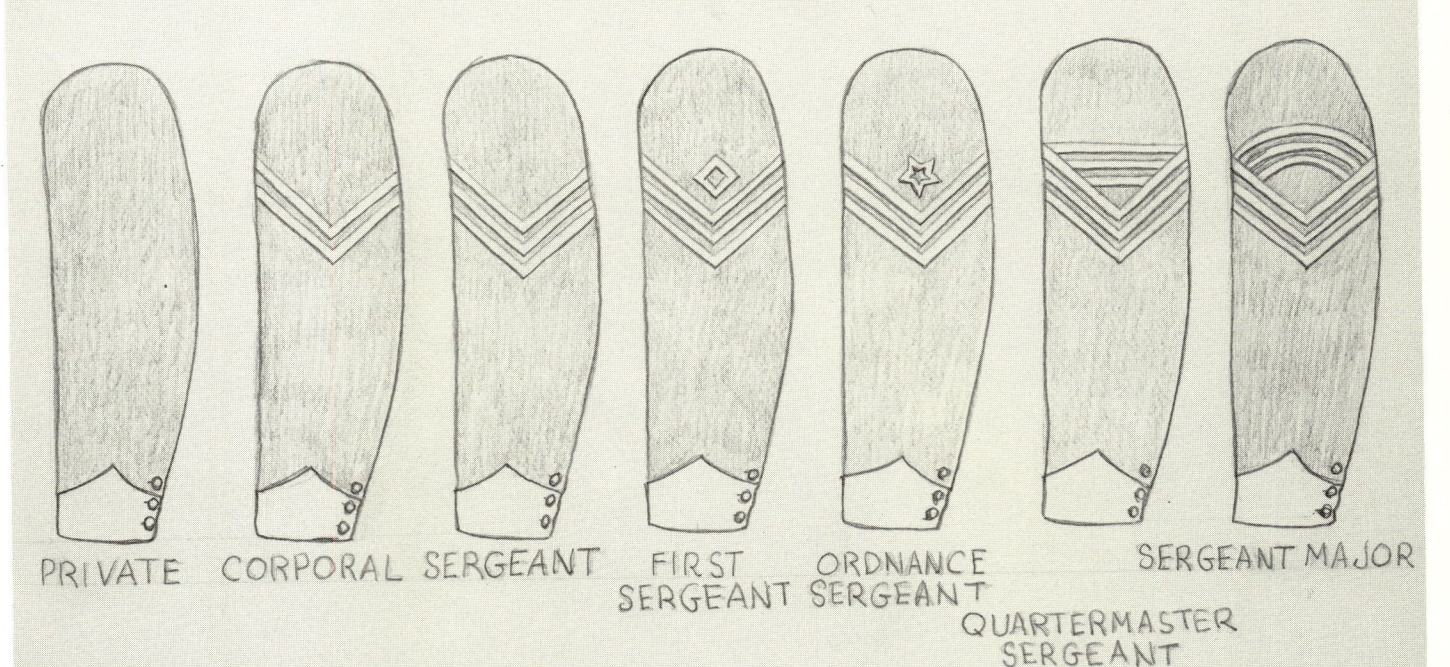

PRIVATE CORPORAL SERGEANT FIRST SERGEANT ORDNANCE SERGEANT QUARTERMASTER SERGEANT SERGEANT MAJOR

Trousers and Shoes

The Confederate soldier had at least the following sources to draw upon for the items in question.

1. Civilian clothing on hand
2. Local militia make-up
3. State issue
4. Confederate army issue
5. Union army issue

From the very start of the war the South captured many U.S. Army quartermaster depots and arsenals located within southern borders. In conjunction with this, the Confederate cavalry captured supply trains and mobile quartermaster stores throughout the war. Finally the stripping of battlefield casualties was a common practice. When one considers the terribley high death rate, this was no mean source of supply. It suggests that "Ole Johnny Reb" could have acquired a a brand new pair of pants and shoes two days before Appomattox.

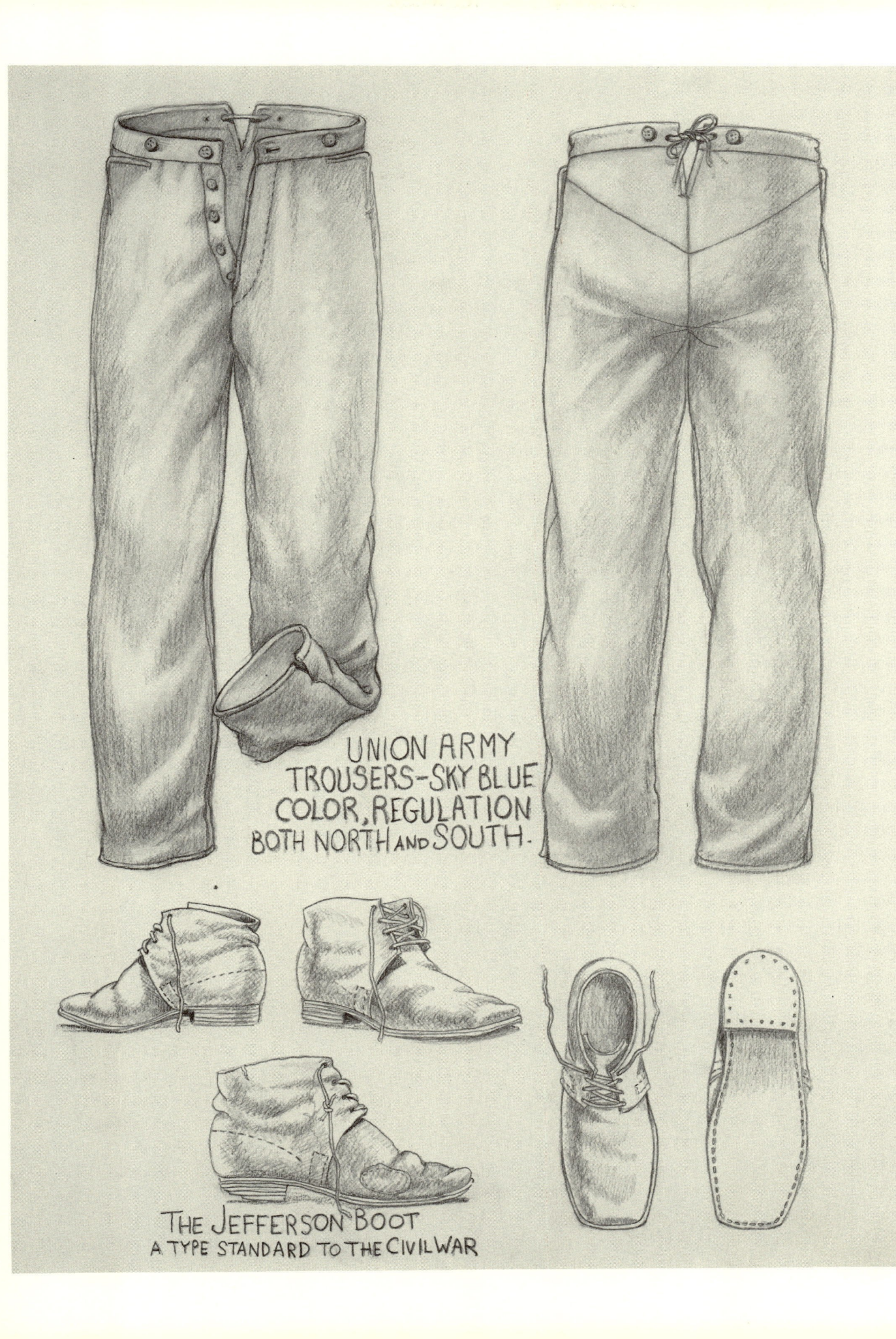

UNION ARMY TROUSERS—SKY BLUE COLOR, REGULATION BOTH NORTH AND SOUTH.

THE JEFFERSON BOOT
A TYPE STANDARD TO THE CIVIL WAR

Belt Plates & Buckles

Officer's two piece sword belt plates →

Possible surviver from the Republic of Texas

Popular enlisted men's belt plates →

Civil War photographs reveal many crude variations of Texan belt plates.

Not all lone star devices were Texan. The grand old Southern states of Florida and Mississippi were known to use it.

Another possible surviver from the Republic of Texas.

One piece frame buckle

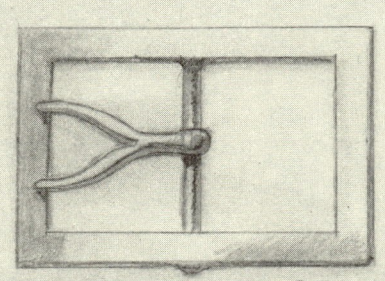

Georgia Forket-Tongue buckle

A most common belt plate, used throughout the Confederacy.

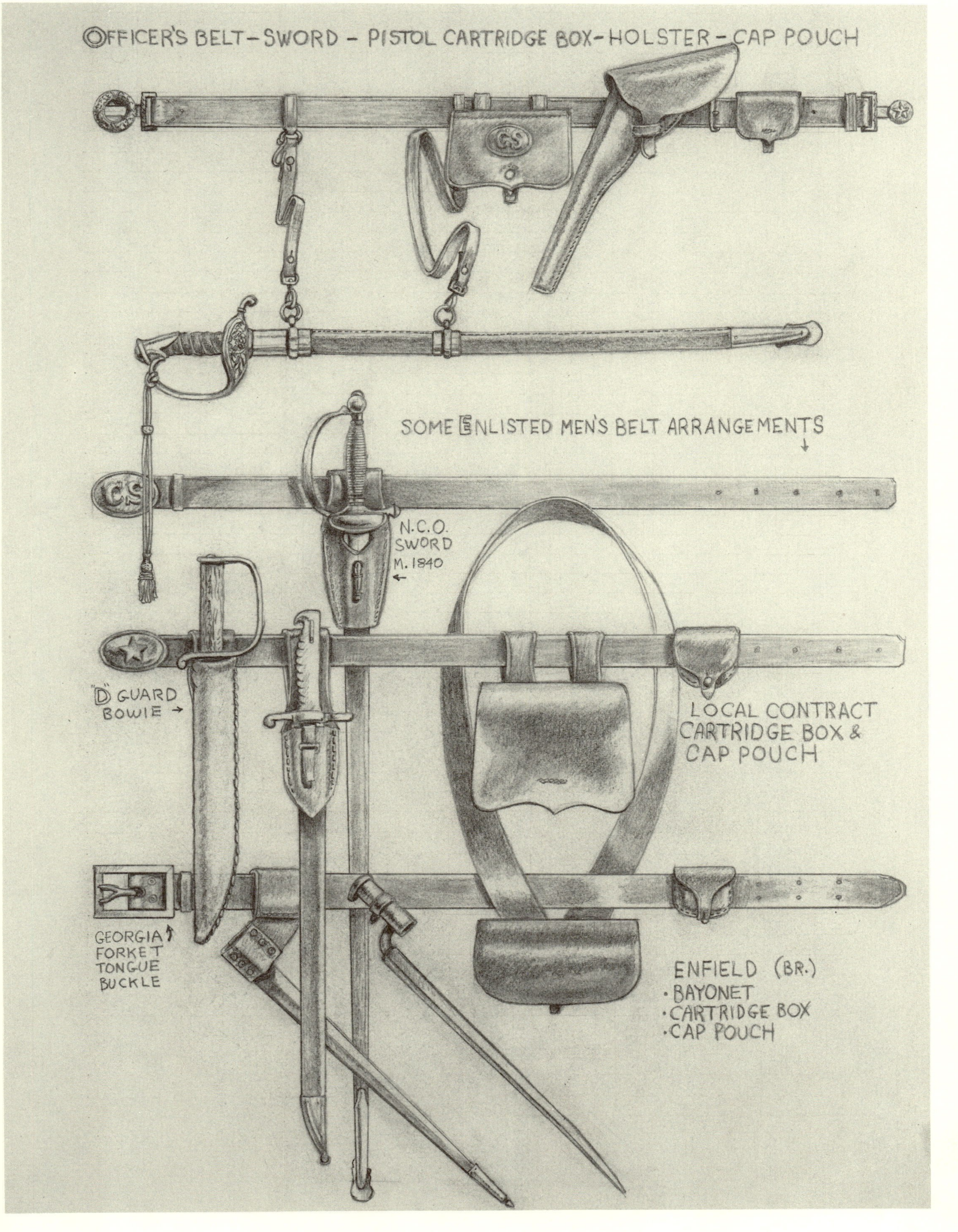

OFFICER'S BELT - SWORD - PISTOL CARTRIDGE BOX - HOLSTER - CAP POUCH
CS
SOME ENLISTED MEN'S BELT ARRANGEMENTS
CS
N.C.O.
SWORD
M. 1840
"D" GUARD
BOWIE
LOCAL CONTRACT
CARTRIDGE BOX &
CAP POUCH
GEORGIA
FORKET
TONGUE
BUCKLE
ENFIELD (BR.)
· BAYONET
· CARTRIDGE BOX
· CAP POUCH

ENFIELD RIFLE MUSKET PATTERN 1853

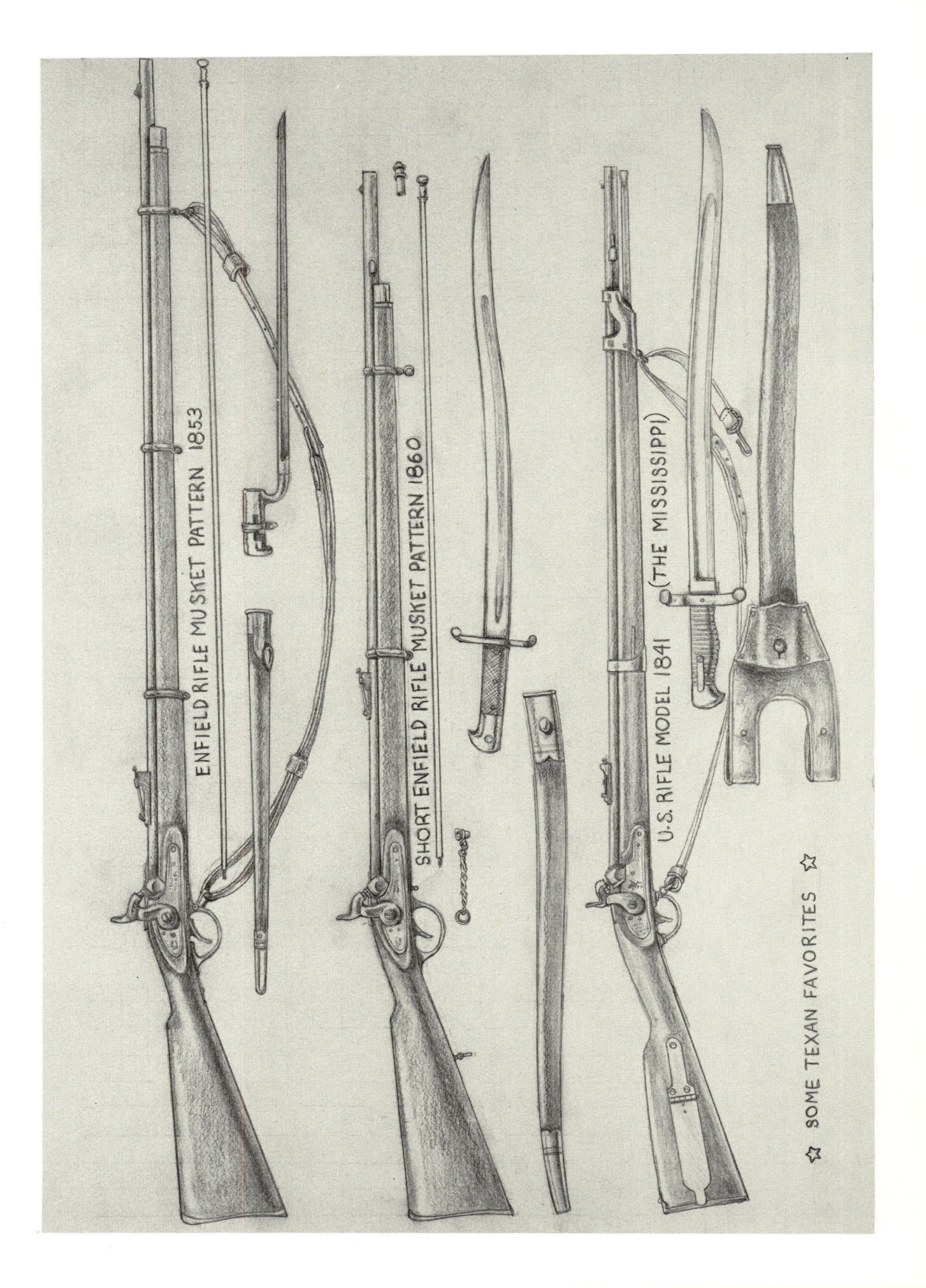

SHORT ENFIELD RIFLE MUSKET PATTERN 1860

U.S. RIFLE MODEL 1841 (THE MISSISSIPPI)

☆ SOME TEXAN FAVORITES ☆

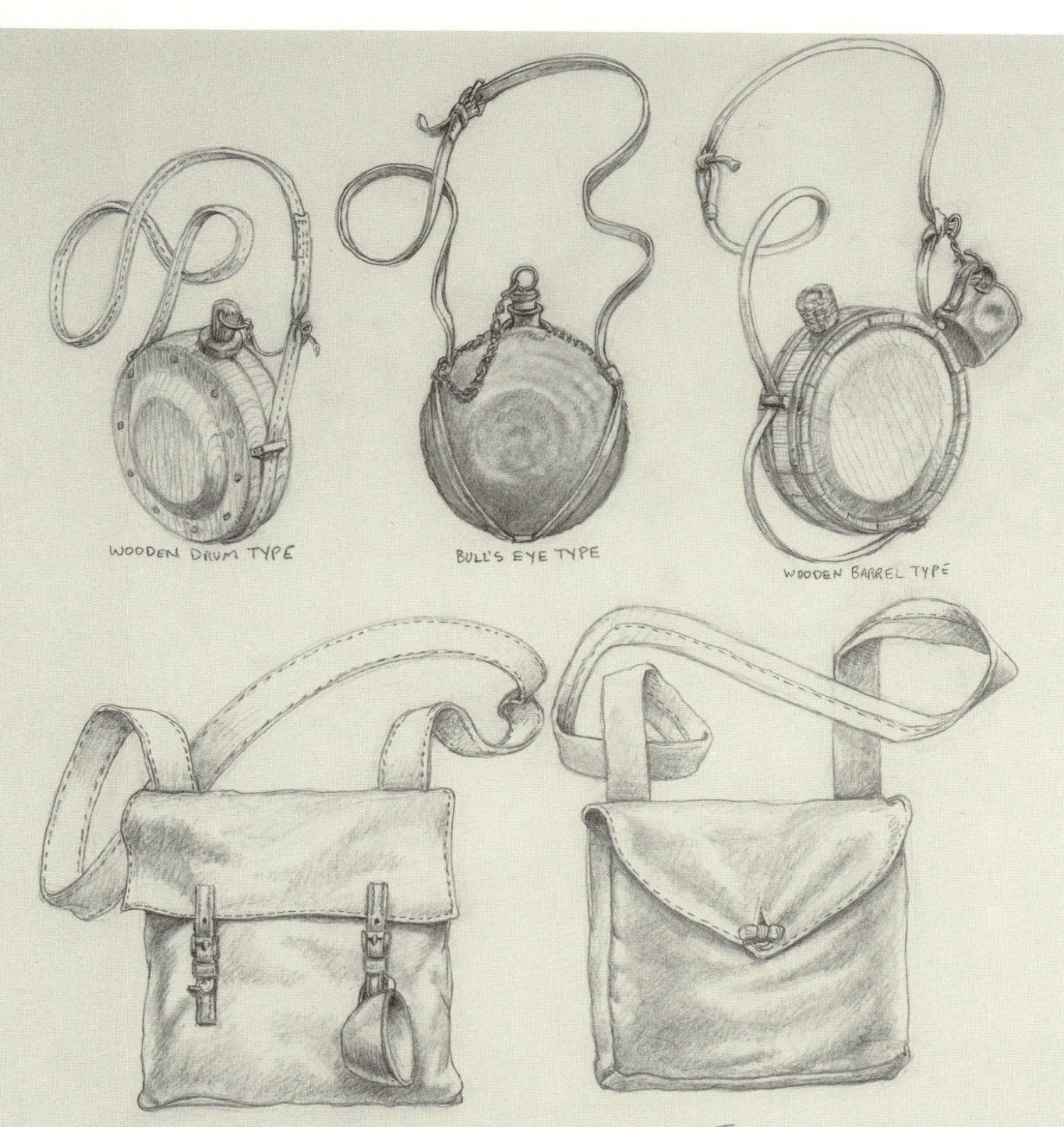

WOODEN DRUM TYPE   BULL'S EYE TYPE   WOODEN BARREL TYPE

Canteens came in many sizes and shapes. The wooden barrel type was quite common and so were the tin drum and bull's eye types. Round and less than eight inches in diameter was the rule. Most of them had canvas slings, but leather was also used. The bull's eye type was usually covered with butternut or gray wool.

Haversacks were among the most useful pieces of equipment that a Civil War soldier had. Usually made of canvas with a removeable canvas liner and canvas shoulder strap. A Confederate soldier's haversack came in many designs and shapes from G.I. Union Army issue to homemade. It was generally about one foot square. Along with his rations the soldier might carry anything he owned in it. Of course he had to keep his greasy bacon away from his spare socks.

SECTION C

BATTLE STANDARDS

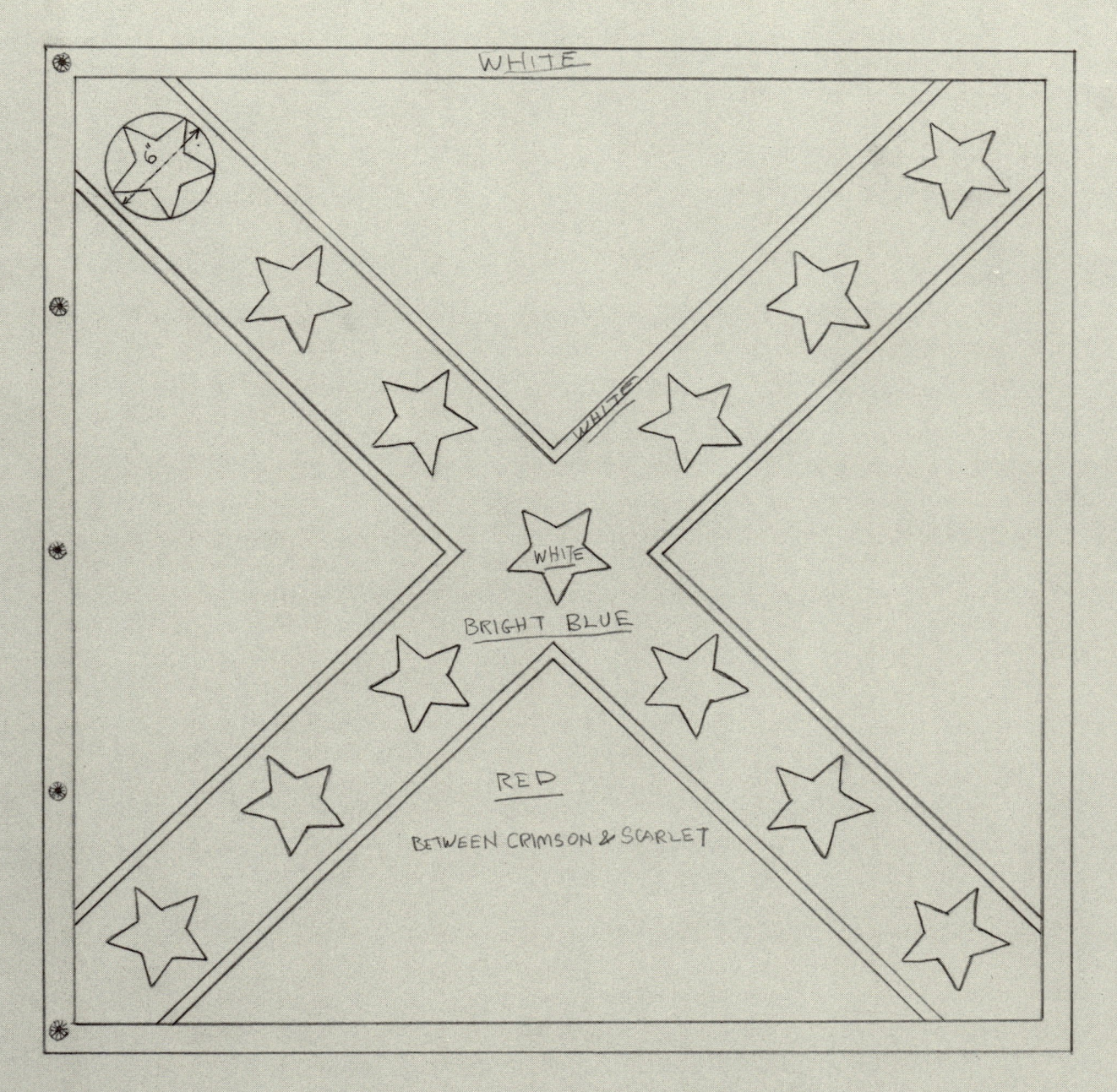

The Regulation Confederate Battle Flag for Infantry

48 inches on the hoist and 48 inches on the fly, exclusive of the border. Blue arms of cross 7½ inches wide. White edging to the cross ½ inch wide. White border around the flag 1½ inch. Total outside measurement 51" x 51". Thirteen white stars are 5 pointed and fit inside a 6 inch circle. Five eyelet holes next to the pole.

THE FIRST BATTLE FLAG OF THE 1ST. TEX. INF. REGT.

THIS FLAG WAS MADE AND PRESENTED TO THE 1ST. TX. INF. REGT. BY MISS LULA WIGFALL, DAU. OF THIS REGT'S. COL., LOUIS T. WIGFALL, IN EARLY 1861. IT WAS FLOWN AT YORKTOWN, ELTHAM'S LANDING, SEVEN PINES, GAINES MILL, MALVERN HILL, FREEMAN'S FORD, THOUROUGHFARE GAP, BOONSBORO GAP, & SHARPSBURG WHERE IT WAS CAPTURED BY PRIVATE SAMUEL JOHNSON OF CO. G. 9TH. PA. RESERVES. THIS WAS IN THE BLOODIEST BATTLE EVER FOUGHT BY AMERICAN SOLDIERS. THE 1ST. TX. SUFFERED THE HIGHEST BATTLE LOSSES EVER SUSTAINED BY ANY AMERICAN REGT. IN ONE DAY. EIGHT TEXANS WERE SHOT DOWN TRYING TO SAVE THIS FLAG.

PVT. JOHNSON, OF THE 9TH. PA., WAS DULY RECOGNIZED FOR THIS MOST EXTRAORDINARY FEAT. HE WAS AWARDED THE MEDAL OF HONOR AND PROMOTED TO A COMMISSIONED OFFICER.

THIS SACRED RELIC WAS RETURNED TO TEXAS IN 1905. IT NOW RESTS IN THE TEXAS STATE ARCHIVES.

Following is an extract from the New York Herald of September 20, 1862:

"While our lines rather faltered the rebels made a sudden and impulsive onset and drove our gallant fellows back over a part of the hard won field. Here, up the hills and down through the woods and standing corn, over the plowed ground and the clover, the line of fire swept to and fro as one side or the other gained a temporary advantage. It is beyond all wonder how men such as these rebel troops are can fight as they do. That those ragged and filthy wretches, sick, hungry and always miserable, should prove such heroes in the fight is past explanation. Men never fought better. There was one regiment that stood up before the fire of two or three of our long range batteries and two full regiments of infantry. Although the air was vocal with the whistle of bullets, there they stood and delivered their fire in perfect order."

SIZE:
FLY — 55½"
HOIST — 56"

THE FLAG OF THE 1st. TX. AFTER THE TWO BATTLE HONORS WERE PAINTED ON IT AND BELOW, AT THE TIME OF ITS CAPTURE AT THE BATTLE OF SHARPSBURG.

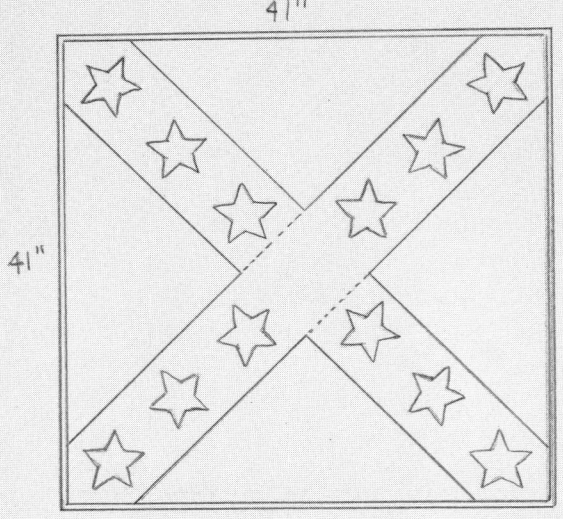

DIMENSIONS

41" X 41" O.A., RED FIELD, LIGHT BLUE CROSS 7 1/4" WIDE, TWELVE WHITE STARS ON 5 1/2" CIRCLE, GOLD BORDER 3/8" WIDE. 37 SMALL NAIL HOLES ON THE HOIST SIDE. STAR SEPARATION: CENTER-1ST; 7 1/2"; CENTER-2ND: 15"; CENTER-3RD: 22 1/2".

THIS FLAG ALONG WITH THE "SEVEN PINES" FLAG WERE RETURNED TO TEXAS IN 1905. THE EVIDENCE IS STRONG THAT THEY WERE BOTH CAPTURED BY PVT. SAMUEL JOHNSON AT THE SAME TIME.

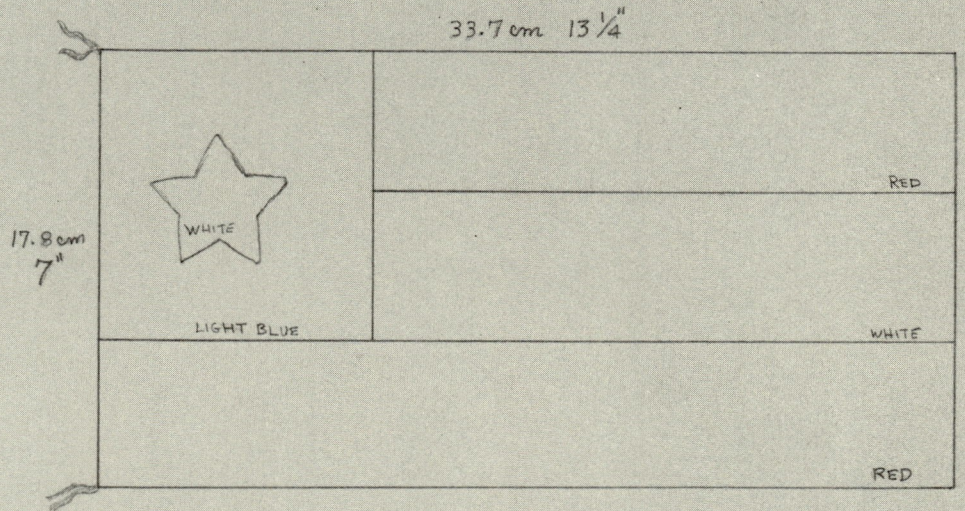

THIS LITTLE FLAG WAS GIVEN TO GEORGE A. BRANARD, COLOR BEARER 1st. TEX., BY SIX YOUNG LADIES IN HOUSTON IN 1862. BRANARD CARRIED THIS FLAG ABOVE THE REGIMENTAL COLORS ON THE SAME STAFF IN ALL OF THE BATTLES UNTIL APPOMATTOX.

THE CONFEDERATE BATTLE FLAG
of the
FOURTH TEXAS VOLUNTEER INFANTRY REGIMENT
HOOD'S TEXAS BRIGADE

    This flag was presented to Colonel (later General) John Bell Hood, Commander of the Fourth Texas Infantry Regiment by Miss Lula Wigfall during November, 1861. Miss Wigfall requested that Colonel Hood in turn present the flag to the Fourth Texas with her compliments. Miss Wigfall was the daughter of Brigadier General Louis T. Wigfall, Commander of the Texas Brigade and later a Senator in the Confederate Congress from Texas. The thirteen stars and the white field of this flag were made from the wedding dress of her mother, who had married General Wigfall in South Carolina twenty-five years before the war. Engraved on the metal spear which capped the flag staff was the following motto: "Fear not, for I am with thee. Say to the North, give up and to the South, keep not back."

    Through the battles of Eltham's Landing, Seven Pines, Gaines' Mill, Freeman's Ford, Second Manassas (Bull Run), Boonsboro Gap, and Sharpsburg (Antietam), this flag waved proudly and victoriously. Nine color bearers fell in battle carrying it. Ed Francis was the first color bearer to carry the Fourth Texas Battle Flag. He carried it through the first four battles before falling seriously wounded at Second Manassas on 30 August 1862. It was at this battle that the spearhead was struck by a minie' ball.

    Pierced by sixty-five bullets and three shells, this historic silken standard was retired October 7, 1862. It was taken back to Texas by Captain (later Colonel) Stephen H. Darden and presented to Governor F. R. Lubbock for deposit in the state archives. After the war was over and the day before the Federal troops reached Austin in 1865, Captain W. C. Walsh and Sergeant R. R. Robertson, members of Company "B", Fourth Texas, who were home at the time, took this flag from the archives in the capital to prevent it from falling into Federal hands. The sacred battle flag was wrapped in a piece of oil cloth and buried on the banks of Barton's Creek near Austin. It remained buried until June 27, 1871 when it was resurrected by a few survivors of Company "B" who had gathered at Barton Springs to celebrate the Ninth Anniversary of the Battle of Gaines' Mill. At Gaines' Mill nearly 300 members of the gallant old Fourth Texas had fallen beneath its folds.

    This banner of "the red field and the blue starry cross" was committed to the custody of Val C. Giles of Austin, a former member of Company "B". Sometime after the turn of the century, it was presented to the United Daughters of the Confederacy and today reposes in their museum located in one corner of the capital grounds at Austin, Texas.

    NOTE: Officially the thirteen stars appearing in the St Andrew's Cross of the Confederate battle flag were of the same size. Each star signified a state that had actually joined the Confederacy or was claimed by the Confederacy such as Kentucky and Missouri. As each state was recognized as being of equal importance thus each star was of equal size. Apparently and naturally Miss Wigfall felt that Texas was the most important state in the Confederacy so she sewed a large star, almost twice the size of the other stars appearing on the banner, as the center star in this Confederate battle flag that she presented to Colonel Hood. To this extent the flag carried by the Fourth Texas did not conform to regulation.

47"

47"

STAR SEPARATION			
FROM CENTER	-1ST:	-2ND:	-3RD:
UPPER STAFF BAR	12"	18½"	25"
LOWER STAFF BAR	11½"	17¾"	24"
UPPER FLY BAR	13½"	19½"	25"
LOWER FLY BAR	13½"	19½"	26"

MATERIAL: SILK

DIMENSIONS
FIELD, PINK (FADED); CROSS, DARK BLUE 6⅜" WIDE; EDGE, WHITE ⅝" WIDE; STARS, WHITE, 12 ON 4" CIRCLES; CENTER STAR, 1 ON 9" CIRCLE; BORDER, YELLOW 2⅜" WIDE ON THREE SIDES, 2¾" WIDE ON STAFF SIDE

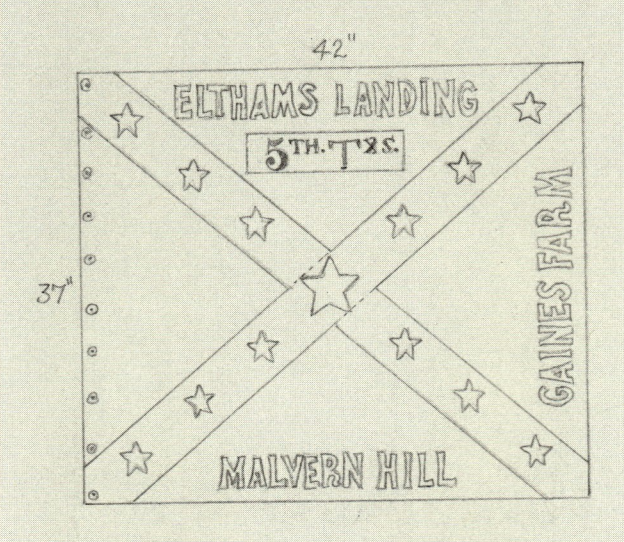

[Flag diagram: 42" wide, 37" tall. Battle honors "ELTHAMS LANDING", "GAINES FARM", "MALVERN HILL". Center designation "5TH. TXS."]

STREAMER – BLUE COTTON WITH ¼" WHITE BORDER.

"VIVERE SAT VINCERE"
OBVERSE: LETTERS WHITE EMBROIDERY 1¾" HIGH.

57¼"
4" 5 REG ☆ VOL
REVERSE: LETTERS & STAR – WHITE WITH RED CHAIN STITCHING OUTLINE.

FIELD: RED; CROSS: DARK BLUE 4½" WIDE; STARS: 13 WHITE, 12 ON 2¼" CIRCLES, ONE ON 5" CIRCLE. MATERIAL: COTTON. ATTACHMENT: TEN WHIPPED EYELETS. STAR SEPARATION: CENTER-1ST: 8"-9"; CENTER-2ND: 14"-16"; CENTER-3RD: 21"-22"-23".

UNIT DESIGNATION
DARK BLUE LETTERS ON WHITE COTTON STRIP 3½" HIGH AND 13" LONG.

BATTLE HONORS
PAINTED IN GOLD LETTERS 2¾" HIGH.

66"

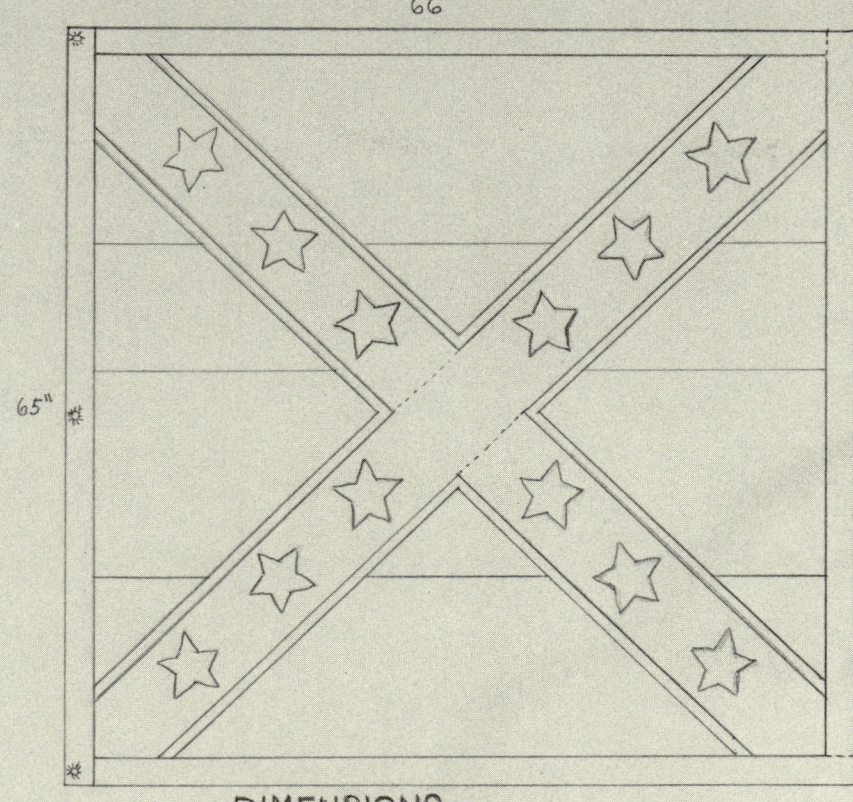

65"

STAR SEPARATION:
CENTER-1ST: 10½";
CENTER-2ND: 20½";
CENTER-3RD: 30½".

DIMENSIONS
65" X 66" O.A., BLUE CROSS 7½" WIDE, STARS ON 6¾" CIRCLES, WHITE EDGE ¾", WHITE BORDER 2½" WIDE, 3 EYELETS.

THIS FLAG WAS CAPTURED AT APPOMATTOX STATION ON APRIL 8, 1865 BY LT. MORTON A. READ CO. D, 8TH. NEW YORK CAVALRY. OF COURSE, LT. READ WAS AWARDED THE MEDAL OF HONOR.

SECTION D

MILITARY STATUETTES

MILITARY STATUETTES

MODEL SOLDIERS HAVE BEEN A MOST POPULAR ART FORM IN ALL CULTURES THROUGHOUT HISTORY. THE SOLDIER HAS ALWAYS STOOD FOR HONOR, BRAVERY AND PATRIOTIC SELF-SACRIFICE. COMBAT VETERANS, FROM ANY ARMY, FORM A BROTHERHOOD THAT IS UNIQUE IN THE ANNALS OF MANKIND.

SHOULD THE READER OF THIS LITTLE SKETCH BOOK DESIRE TO CREATE ONE OF HOOD'S PEOPLE, I HAVE INCLUDED PLANS FOR FOUR FIGURES. THEY CAN BE CARVED IN WOOD OR STONE OR MODELED IN ANY OF THE CLAYS OR WAXES. MY PREFERENCE IS TO CARVE THEM FROM BASSWOOD. THE LACK OF GRAIN AND THE LIGHT TONE IS IDEAL FOR DETAIL AND COLOR.

A GOOD WAY TO GET STARTED IS TO TRACE BOTH FRONT AND BACK OF THE DRAWINGS ONTO THE WOOD. BANDSAW THE OUTLINE, BUT NOT TOO CLOSE. NEXT, PENCIL IN BOTH RIGHT AND LEFT SIDES. CARVE OUT THE MAJOR FORMS FIRST AND THEN RE-PENCIL THE PIECE. THE OLD WOODCARVER'S CLICHÉ OF "JUST CUT AWAY WHAT YOU DON'T WANT" APPLIES HERE.

THE ORIGINAL DRAWINGS ARE 18" TALL, YOU CAN ENLARGE OR REDUCE THE SKETCH BOOK DRAWINGS, BY XEROX, TO SUIT YOUR NEED.

GOOD LUCK,

Tom

PRIVATE 1861
1ST TEXAS INF., C.S.A.

TOM JONES

REGIMENTAL
SERGEANT MAJOR

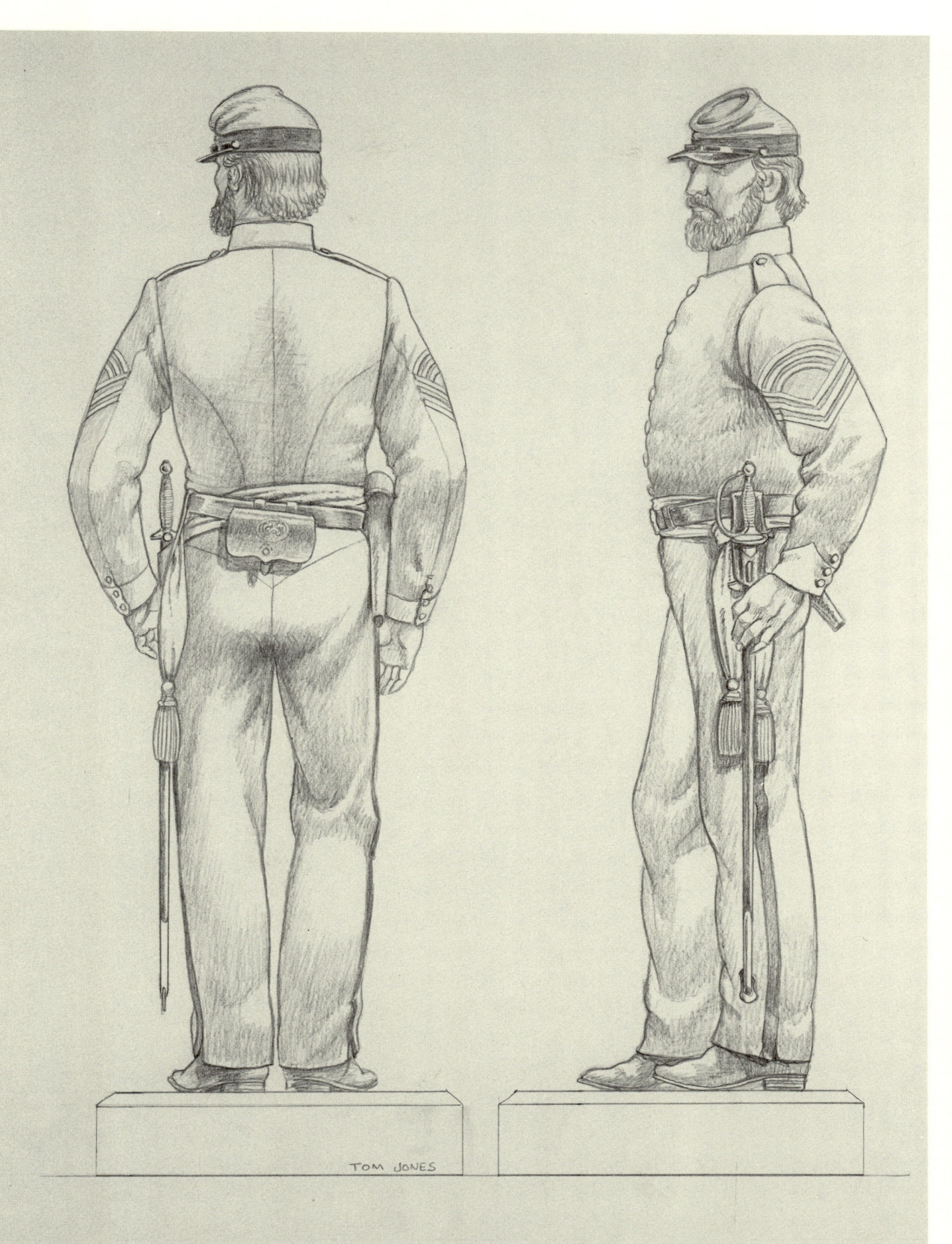

TOM JONES

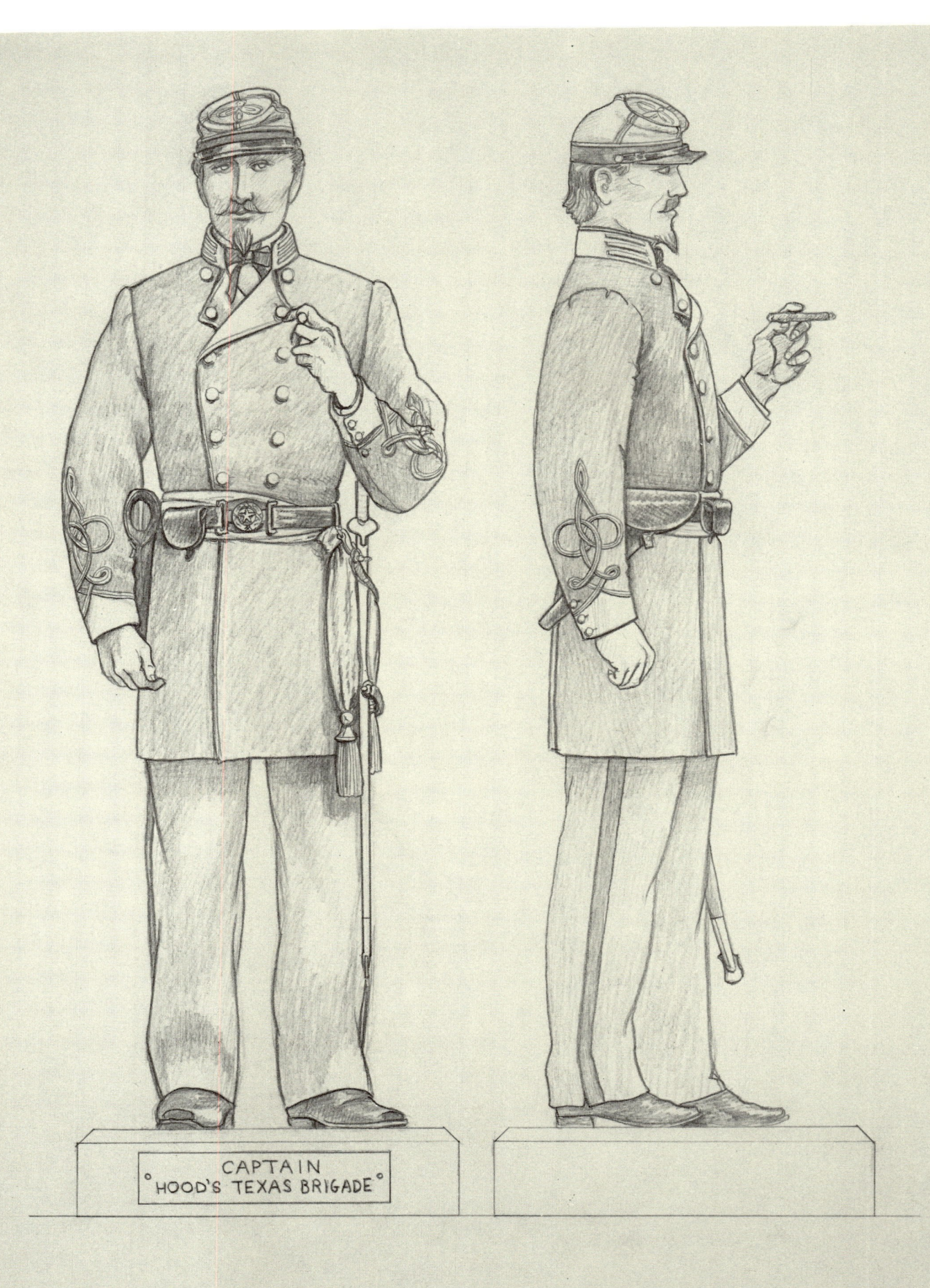

CAPTAIN
"HOOD'S TEXAS BRIGADE"

COLOR

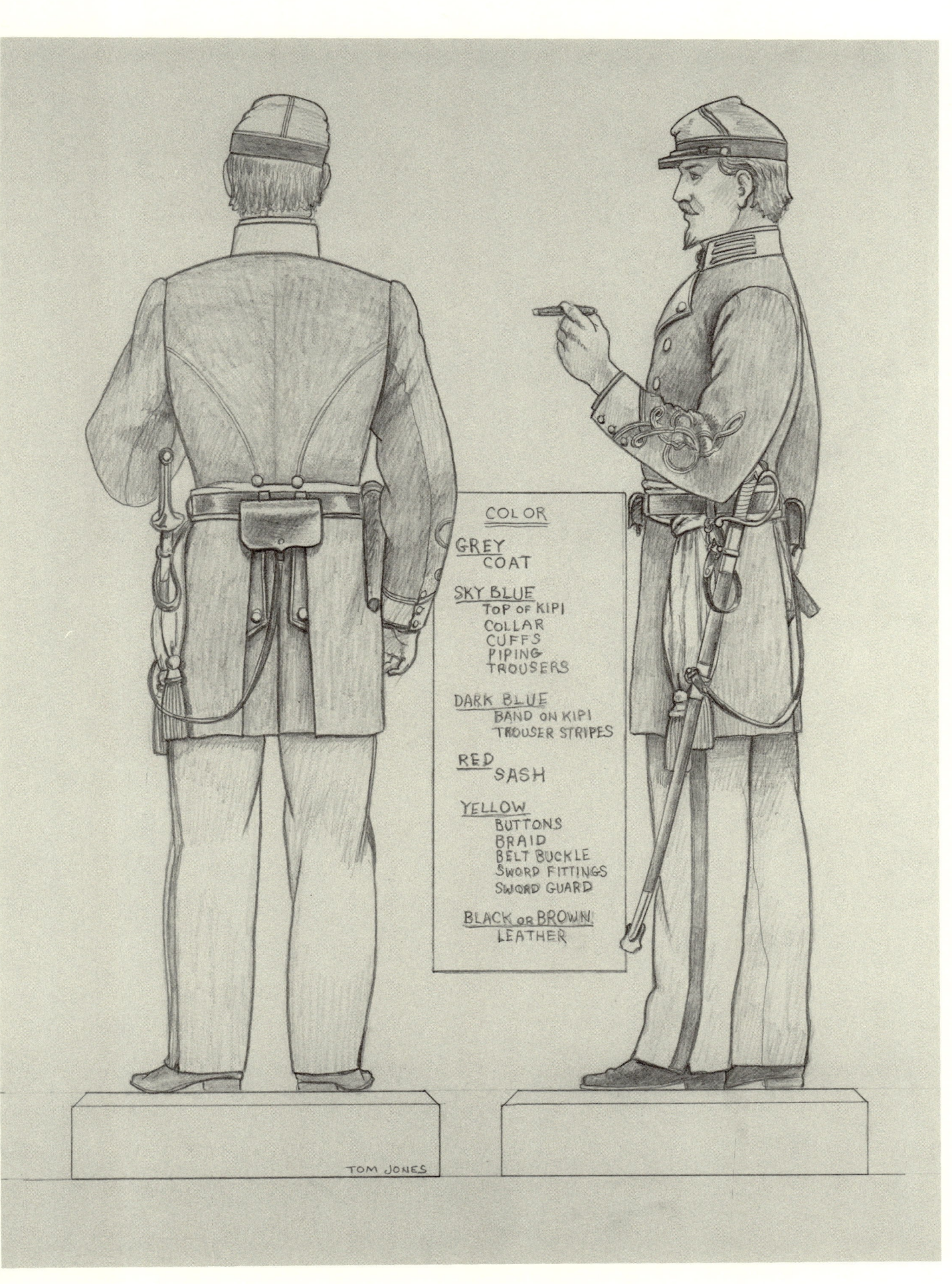

<u>GREY</u>
COAT

<u>SKY BLUE</u>
TOP OF KIPI
COLLAR
CUFFS
PIPING
TROUSERS

<u>DARK BLUE</u>
BAND ON KIPI
TROUSER STRIPES

<u>RED</u> SASH

<u>YELLOW</u>
BUTTONS
BRAID
BELT BUCKLE
SWORD FITTINGS
SWORD GUARD

<u>BLACK or BROWN</u>
LEATHER

TOM JONES

THE BITTER END
1865

Tom Jones

Friends of the Houston Public Library

R0124768010 txrra   T
                     973
                     .7464
                     J79

Jones, Tom, 1920-
Tom Jones' Hood's Texas
    Brigade sketch book

Houston Public Libraries
FOR LIBRARY USE ONLY